LAUNCHING MISSIONAL SERMON-BASED SMALL GROUPS

INTEGRATING WORSHIP, FORMATION AND SERVICE

DR. DOUG CUSHING

www.pinnlead.com/pl-press

ISBN:

ACKNOWLEDGEMENTS

The late South African Archbishop, Desmond Tutu once said: "You don't choose your family. They are God's gift to you, as you are to them." I am so grateful to be part of a number of different families that have inspired and blessed me as I wrote this book. The first family I want to thank are my colleagues at Pinnacle Leadership, and especially Mark Tidsworth, for their koinonia, encouragement and witness to the gospel. In many ways, my Pinnacle colleagues serve as my 'church family.'

The second family I am indebted to are the Covenant Partners of the church that I am honored to serve, the Bridge Presbyterian Church in Leland, NC. They accept me; support me; pray for me and allow me the space to be what God has created me to be. Our ongoing experiment with missional sermon-based small groups has been essential to the writing of this book.

I also want to thank my nuclear family. I am immeasurably grateful to my 85-year-old parents – whose lifetime of faithfulness to the Lord has shaped my love and serve Jesus Christ. I thank my two brothers, Tim and Brett, who love me unconditionally and pray for my work. To my wife, Sharon, I am grateful for the generous freedom you give me to write and the unwavering encouragement you offer me.

I give thanks to God for my brothers in Christ, Jeff Gilstrap and Adam Ashcraft, who have encouraged me along the way. I am deeply indebted to my editor and friend, Ralph Jeffrey, who worked closely with me offering gentle feedback and friendship.

Most of all, I am grateful to the One who has adopted me into the household of God; who has blessed me with a calling to pastoral ministry and who uses my very ordinary gifts for extraordinary purpose.

You all are God's gift to me!   Doug

FOREWORD

I can clearly remember meeting Doug Cushing for the first time. The deep, rich, vibration of his "made for radio" voice, combining with his clear midwestern accent, made me want to listen to him all day long. Looking back over the last seventeen years of ongoing partnership in the Way of Jesus, my ears still perk up when Doug speaks.

Now, looking back, it's clear to me that I'm interested in listening to Doug for deeper reasons than his excellent and pleasant speaking voice. It's Doug's authentic, consistent, and ongoing appetite for God that draws me toward him. I've watched him lead the church he started in South Carolina toward spiritual maturity. I've watched Doug lead that church through several identity and size transitions. I've watched Doug realize that call was completed, opening himself and his family to a new calling. I've watched Doug partner with people in Leland, NC to start and develop this new thriving church called The Bridge. Through each of these experiences, I've seen Doug at his best...and worst (yes, he's experienced dry spells). But I've yet to see Doug's commitment to Christ waver.

I share this with you because you need to know this book, Launching Missional Sermon-Based Small Groups, comes from a person who's deeply involved in this Christian Movement. Like all effective ministry, the movement described in this book comes from the movement of God in a disciple's spirit and experience. I'm glad more Christ-followers can now experience the person and faith of Doug Cushing through this new book.

Beyond encountering Doug as a person and disciple of Jesus, I'm excited about this book in another huge way. Through Pinnacle Leadership Associates, Doug, myself, and our other Associates have the privilege of engaging with such a variety of churches and their leaders.

As we do this ministry, I cannot track how many times we are asked how to integrate worship, formation, and service. Church leaders are recognizing the disconnects between these aspects of our faith lives, wishing greater focus was possible. "How can we connect worship, what we are engaging in small groups, and how we serve in our church and community?" O, let me count the various ways I've heard this question over the last ten years. As familiar church paradigms in North America continue to deconstruct, new expressions of church are rising to fill the vacuum. This book describes a clear pathway for living into the Way of Jesus in culturally relevant, while also faithful, ways.

At the risk of delaying your engagement a moment longer, I'm very happy to lift up the fact that this book is extremely practical. Doug is a practitioner of our faith. Beyond that Doug is a pastor who is keenly focused on developing disciples. From that perspective, Doug generously shares the insights and practices gained through real life ministry in God's vineyard. You will find practical guidance for each stage of your effort to bring missional sermon-based small groups to the life of your church.

Now when we at Pinnacle are frequently asked the question noted above, we have an answer. "Read this book as quick as you can, finding an excellent way to develop disciples and engage with God's mission in this Postmodern world."

Thank you Doug Cushing and blessings to every reader as you engage the stirring and exciting possibilities found on these pages.

Rev. Mark E. Tidsworth
Founder and Team Leader
Pinnacle Leadership Associates
Chapin, South Carolina
March 31, 2023

TABLE OF CONTENTS

CHAPTER ONE

AT THE INTERSECTION OF LONGING AND URGENCY

INTRODUCTION

What did we just do? It was late March 2020 and the elders of our church unanimously agreed to close the doors of the church I serve as pastor. Driving home, I kept saying the same thing: "Did we just do that...close down our church's facilities until further notice? Wait, did we just agree to suspend in-person Sunday worship? Did we just vote to cease all small group gatherings?"

Every pastor and lay person can relate to the surreal events triggered by a pandemic that swept through our world leaving in its path death, destruction, fatigue and change. Of all the changes brought on by the pandemic, few were as unprecedented and gut-wrenching for church leaders as the decision to suspend in-person worship and 'go virtual.' Even if your church didn't suspend in-person worship, your congregation probably experienced a steep decline of in-person worship.

According to Pew Research, in July 2020, roughly four months after COVID-19 upended life in America, 13% of U.S. adults reported having attended religious services in person during the previous month. That rose to 17% in March 2021 and then to 26% in September 2021, and (as of this writing) stands at 27%.

Over the same period, the share of Americans who say they have streamed religious services online or watched them on TV in the past month declined from 36% in July 2020 to 28% in September 2021 and is currently at 30%.

About a third of U.S. adults (32%) in the March 2022 survey say they *typically* go to religious services at least once or twice a month. Of these self-described regular attenders, two-thirds (67%) report that they actually have attended physically (in person) in the last month, while 57% say they have watched services online or on TV during that period.[1]

The pandemic supercharged a disturbing trend that church leaders already knew, but were somewhat reluctant to admit. Fewer and fewer Americans are participating in Christian worship. Years ago, the Barna Group found that more than 90 percent of Americans say they believe in God. Many of them will say their faith is important to them. Yet, just 43 percent said they had attended church the week they were surveyed.[2] The pandemic has only accelerated the rate of decline in worship attendance.

Additionally, the pandemic brought into stark relief the growing disconnect among Americans who express faith in God yet are reluctant to participate in a local church. While this disconnect was generally recognized by most pastors, the pandemic is forcing church leaders and congregations to face it head-on.

Prior to the pandemic, I knew many talented and dedicated pastors who lived and served in churches that were declining in vitality, resources and members, even while spirituality was on the rise in America.[3] Making matters worse for my pastor-friends was a sense of inevitability that the church in America would continue to decline.

1   Justin Nortey, "More Houses of Worship Are Returning to Normal, But In-Person Worship Remains Unchanged Since Fall," *Pew Research Center*, March 22, 2022, <https://www.pewresearch.org/fact-tank/2022/03/22/more-houses-of-worship-are-returning-to-normal-operations-but-in-person-attendance-is-unchanged-since fall/#:~:text=In%20July%202020%2C%20roughly%20four.and%20now%20stands%20at%2027%25.>
2   Charles Dennison, *Mainline Manifesto: The Inevitable New Church* (St. Louis: Charlice Press, 2005), xi.
3   Michael Lipka and Claire Gecewicz, 2017, Pew Research Center: accessed June 7, 2022, <http://www.pewresearch.org/fact-tank/2017/09/06/more-americans-now-say-they-re-spiritual-but-not-religious/>

However, while many of my ordained colleagues grieved the change in the religious landscape in America, they grieved as people not without hope. Time and again in my coaching and consulting practice through Pinnacle Leadership Associates, I listened to pastors who longed for a different, more robust way of doing and being church. Yet, they were constrained by congregations resistant to change and reticent to experiment with innovative ways of being church. The disruption of worship caused by the pandemic has created an openness to fresh ideas and an urgent window of opportunity for congregations to explore new ways of doing and being church.

Are you one of those pastors who has faithfully waited and hoped for the fresh winds of the Holy Spirit to blow across our nation and bring renewal to the Church? And now, as you lead your congregation through the uncharted waters of a post-pandemic world, are you wondering if this is a Kairos-moment; a time when the conditions are right to experiment with creative, fresh expressions of the church?

It's not only pastors who yearn for a new, Spirit-infused way of being church to the world. Many of the faithful who sit in the pews; fill the choir lofts; sing in the praise bands and lead Bible studies long for the same thing. I've always wondered why these dedicated saints stay active in church. Are they motivated to stay by a guilt-induced sense of responsibility? Is it a fear of divine punishment that keeps the faithful coming back week after week? Or maybe, just maybe, it's an indomitable sense of hope in our triune God?

Despite the obvious decline in the church in North America and the disruptive confusion caused by the pandemic, I am convinced that deep within God's people, the Spirit is stirring up a longing for something more; something different. I believe the Spirit is birthing a hunger within our congregations for something more than the normal church encounter; something beyond an hour-a-week worship experience that is *siloed* from the rest of life. In fact, the growth of virtual worship is forcing churches to consider how their mission can impact the world outside their walls and on days not called Sunday.

Do you feel that stirring? Do you? Are you one of those dedicated pastors or faithful disciples of Jesus who are committed to staying in the church regardless of the ongoing decline and despite the impact of the pandemic? Is your commitment to stay in the Church fueled by a deep longing for a different, more robust way of doing and being church.

Here's some good news. That longing is not just limited to the people who faithfully worship every Sunday. Our risen Lord is at work within people who have left the church as well. Could it be that many of those folks we refer to as un-churched or de-churched are not anti-church but anti-church-of-their-past?[4] Could it be that deep in their soul, they too long to be part of a community of God's people who seek to follow in the way of Jesus vigorously and authentically?

Pastors who lead our churches; faithful disciples who fill our churches and seekers on the margins of our churches are all yearning for a Church eager to bear witness to the coming reign of God and hungry to follow in Jesus' Kingdom ways. And the disruptions and chaos caused by the pandemic are catalyzing churches and leaders into action.

The pre- and post-pandemic challenge for church leaders remains the same. Only now, after more than two turbulent years of disruption and bedlam, there is an urgency accompanying that challenge.

For many believers and seekers, the challenge is not just the call to follow in the way of Jesus and live a life distinct from culture but, rather, to find a church where they can learn to do so faithfully, winsomely and within a community of like-minded disciples. Is that what you are looking for? Is that what you want your church to embody?

---

4   Patrick Vaughn, *Meeting Jesus at Starbucks: Good News for Those Done With Church* (Columbia: Pinnacle Leadership Press, 2018).

Not surprisingly, this is what Jesus longs for in His church as well. In Matthew 5: 13 – 16, we learn that what Jesus longs for in his relationship with His people is for us to live radically different lives than the world around us; to live lives that show forth the reality of Jesus, alive within us, and that show forth God's will and intention for the world. And…to do so together, in community.

This is why Jesus says to us in Matthew's gospel: "You are the salt of the earth and you are the light of the world." Notice he does not say: You should be salt or the light nor does he say you could be if you only do these specific things. Jesus is saying that this is who we are because our Lord has taken up residence within us. The light of Christ is already within us.[5]

I was a sprinter on my college track team. My coach once said: "Doug, some day you are going to run a sub-fifty second 400-meter dash." When I told him there was no way I could do that, he replied: "Doug, it's already within you." My coach helped me learn what was already within me. The light of Jesus is already within us. God has put his Spirit within us and given us a new nature.

So, Jesus longs for us to learn his ways and discover how the light of Christ already radiates from us. The purpose of this book is to share the innovative model for small groups that we, at the Bridge Presbyterian Church, have used to help our Covenant Partners[6] tap into this deep longing I've just described.

At the Bridge Presbyterian Church, disciples have discovered a robust and authentic faith through the unique way in which our shared life integrates worship, fellowship, prayer, Christian formation and mission through the formation of missional sermon-based small groups. Guided by our mission statement along with our unique adaptation of

5   M. Scott Boren, *Missional Small Groups: Becoming A Community That Makes a Difference in the World* (Grand Rapids: Baker Books, 2010), chapter 3.
6   Covenant Partners is the name we use at the Bridge Presbyterian Church to refer to what other churches call church members.

15

sermon-based small groups, we are creating vibrant, missional-minded disciples eager to worship weekly; share life together in small groups and join Jesus on mission in our neighborhood.

Before I share our innovative twist for doing sermon-based small groups, I need to provide you with a little context. What follows is a brief description of our new church and a story highlighting how the Holy Spirit worked through our sermon-based small groups to bring missional energy and spiritual vitality to our young congregation.

I serve as the Pastor and head of staff of the Bridge Presbyterian Church. As I write, we are an eight-year-old newer worshiping community of the Presbyterian Church (USA). Prior to the pandemic, we held two worship services each Sunday in a storefront (although we have just purchased a new building and property and are in the process of moving as I write this book). Additionally, the Bridge is blessed with a talented and creative church staff along with dedicated lay leaders whom we call Elders.

Our steady, pre-pandemic growth allowed us to charter – which means we became financially self-sufficient and no longer needed assistance from our higher governing body: the Presbytery. Additionally, our growth forced us to move to a new and expanded rental space – which doubled the size of our facilities. While many refer to the Bridge as a successful new church (whatever that means), the truth is that the joys and struggles of our emerging new congregation mirror those of many church plants across the country.

The Bridge Presbyterian Church is in Leland NC. Leland is a small, but fast-growing bedroom suburb of the coastal city of Wilmington, NC. With its proximity to the Brunswick County beaches; its low taxes; nine months of nearly ideal weather and affordable housing, Leland has become an attractive destination to relocate. People from up and down the eastern seaboard are discovering and moving to one of the amenity-rich planned communities popping up around Leland.

All this growth has, predictably, created some consternation among the small contingent of long-time Leland residents who feel like the town they have called home all their lives no longer feels like home. Long-time residents resist the inevitable changes taking place and resent the modern strip centers; the new restaurants; the trendy shops and the increased traffic.

This has created a widening rift between what some refer to as Old Leland and New Leland. While many in our growing suburb are completely unaware of the fissure, the members of the mission team at the Bridge Presbyterian Church were dialed into the discord between Old and New Leland. And to their credit, members of the mission team wanted to do something about it.

In the spring of 2017, I listened in on a discussion our mission team was having about this rift within the community. Their question was what, if anything, is our new church called to do about this ever-widening chasm. Listening to this conversation, I was stuck by the fact that the team was, without realizing it, wrestling with a call from God to work for peace and reconciliation in our community.

Recognizing the stirring of the Holy Spirit, I volunteered to lead a bible study on the theological and biblical foundation for peacemaking. One month later, I stood in front of the mission team members and presented a Bible study titled: <u>A Reformed Understanding of Peacemaking</u>. Something unexpected happened during that study. It was what my friend, Dr. Andrew Purves describes as: "The Holy Spirit showing up."[7]

By the end of the study, everyone in room had a clear, palpable sense that the Lord was calling the Bridge into a deeper understanding of peacemaking. The team unanimously recommended to our session

---

7   Andrew Purves, *The Crucifixion of Ministry: Surrendering Our Ambition to the Service of Christ* (Downers Grove: InterVarsity Press, 2007), 9.

(that's the name we Presbyterians give to our leadership team of elders) that I lead a four-week, church-wide study on the biblical basis for peacemaking. Not only did our session approve the recommendation, but they asked that I create a sermon series around this topic for our fall sermon-based small group session.

That summer, we engaged in four ninety-minute sessions. Each session was punctuated with lively discussion, prayer and discernment. That fall, I lead a nine-week sermon series titled: Seeking the Welfare of Our City. The first three weeks explored God's call in Jeremiah to the Jewish exiles in Babylonian captivity to seek the welfare (or shalom) of the city. The final six weeks looked at how Nehemiah worked for the welfare of his city by rebuilding the walls and gates of Jerusalem.

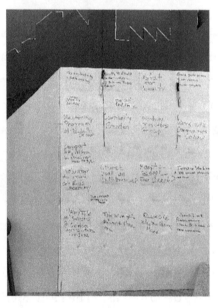

Each sermon in the series explored different facets of working for the welfare or the shalom of the city. Each week, six different sermon based small groups met to discuss the scripture passages and questions I created in the weekly sermon-based small group study guide.

Additionally, we created a simple but effective set design that we erected along the wall behind our band. The set design was a generic silhouette of a city skyline. In front of the sky line there was a painted stone wall - which symbolized Nehemiah's rebuilding efforts in Jerusalem.

At the conclusion of the fourth week of the series, folks were invited to pick up a Sharpie and write on one of the stones how they felt the

Lord was calling their small group to seek the shalom or welfare of our city. By the end of the series all the stones had been scribbled on.

Through the weekly rhythm of worship and sermon-based small groups, we experienced an increase of creative, Spirit-infused ideas flowing throughout our young congregation. The energy and passion of folks at the Bridge was palpable in worship. The Holy Spirit was, without question, creating an unmistakable passion within God's people at the Bridge to seek the welfare of our city.

And the most exciting part of that particular missional sermon-based small group series was what happened at the conclusion of the sermon series. Further on, I'll share how people in the small groups were used by the Holy Spirit to make a difference in the neighborhoods around our church.

I share this story with you not to brag. In reality, I didn't do much except get out of the way of the Holy Spirit. I share this story with you because this sort of experience is exactly what many of us, pastors and lay people, pray and dream might happen in our sanctuaries and worship centers. Who among us, doesn't dream of being part of a congregation seeking to discuss how to seek God's shalom for their city?

Who among us, doesn't pray to be part of a congregation passionately committed to joining Jesus in extending God's Kingdom by working for peace, justice and reconciliation in the neighborhood? Who among us, doesn't long to be part of a gathering of God's people who are seriously committed to taking the gospel, in word and deed, into the heart of their community?

And, perhaps, the best part of this story is that neither I, (as their pastor) nor the elders were initiating, manipulating, cajoling, inspiring, or leading any of this! The Holy Spirit was clearly and decisively leading our young congregation organically; from the bottom up. We were simply "hitching a ride with where the Lord was leading."[8] This

8   Purves, *The Crucifixion of Ministry*, 10.

entire transformation occurred because the Holy Spirit lit a fire under our new church and

the way the people of the Bridge caught fire was through the unique way we integrated worship, Christian formation, prayer, fellowship and mission through our missional sermon-based small group ministry.

Prior to the pandemic, I would often share that story while leading workshops on how to make the shift to missional sermon-based small group. It was not uncommon that the story was met with a mixture of excitement and resistance by those in the room. Those in the workshop weren't resisting the idea of missional small groups. Instead, they knew that making the shift to become a church of missional sermon-based small groups would not be easy, and in some cases, would be unwelcome within their congregations.

Long-established practices of Sunday morning adult Sunday school and long-held views of what should and should not happen during Sunday worship, stood in the way of the sort of shift I was inviting congregations and leaders to consider during my workshops.

After two-plus years of the pandemic disrupting the habits and practices of our churches, I wonder if there is a new openness (and/or urgency) within congregations to consider fresh ways of being the church. I wonder if there is a need in post-pandemic congregations to unite the virtual and in-person Sunday worshipers through small groups? I wonder if the scope, size and vision of missional sermon-based small groups might be the perfect 'holy experiment'[9] for the post-pandemic church in North America.

When I look back on how the Holy Spirit powerfully moved through our congregation during Seeking the Welfare of The City sermon-based small group series, I realized that all the energy, creativity and all the concrete missional initiatives that were launched in the small groups,

---

9   Author and Pinnacle Leadership partner, David Brown uses this phrase in his forthcoming book: *How To Design Holy Experiments In Your Church And Community.*

didn't happen by accident. Additionally, all the missional vitality didn't happen in a vacuum. From the very beginning of our new church, structures and processes were created that helped birth a culture that would support and sustain this sort of robust missional experience of the Holy Spirit.

In the following chapters, I will outline how to develop and launch missional sermon-based small groups in your congregation along with how to seamlessly integrate your small groups into the larger structures, systems and mission statement of your church. My hope is to guide you through a process that will foster renewal and inspire a new way of being church in the world while also creating a robust life of faith for your congregation as it struggles to find its footing in a post-COVID environment and beyond. But for now, let me tell you about what happened at *-the conclusion of the <u>Seeking the Welfare of Our City</u> series.

After we wrapped-up our sermon-based small group study on <u>Seeking the Welfare of Our City</u>, we invited the congregation to gather for two separate gatherings. The purpose was to pray, discuss and discern where the Spirit was leading us and what would be our next steps.

We tasked an elder in our session to drive the discernment process. He didn't really need to drive anything, because the Spirt had already been fostering a passion within our congregation to make a difference in our neighborhood. Those nine small group sessions inspired a number of people at the Bridge to launch new and exciting ministries with the sole purpose of being a blessing, the tangible touch of God to our neighbors.[10]

Among the new initiatives that gained traction in our congregation, was a vision to partner with a new food pantry being launched in

---

10   Hugh Halter and Matt Smay, *The Tangible Kingdom Primer* (Gig Harbor: Missio Publishing, 2009) 11.

our neighborhood through an organization called Brunswick Family Assistance. Currently a number of couples in our congregation volunteer there weekly.

Another emerging mission initiative birthed from our Seeking the Welfare of the City small group series was a developing partnership with the Brunswick County School district. Inspired by the Holy Spirit working within his small group, one Covenant Partner of the Bridge worked to launch a Best Kids program. Folks at the Bridge began volunteering in the Best Kids Program with the goal of helping all children in Brunswick County become fluent readers by the end of the third grade.

This story is an example of the fruit that one missional sermon-based small group series bore in our shared life at the Bridge Presbyterian Church. But none of that would have happened without our unique brand of missional sermon-based small groups being in place.

For much of the rest of this book, I intend to describe the small group ministry at the Bridge. My goal will be to describe the innovative ways our small groups are integrating; a) how we worship; with b) how we grow disciples; with c) how we join Jesus on mission and how we align all of that with our church mission statement. And then, help you navigate your path toward making this shift.

However, the more I thought about this chapter, the more I realized that our small groups are not the focus of our shared life at the Bridge Presbyterian Church. Small groups are simply a mechanism or a channel for helping God's people at the Bridge join in Jesus' work of extending the Kingdom of God to our neighborhood.

Joining Jesus in Extending the Kingdom of God into Our Neighborhood

The phrase: "Joining Jesus in extending the Kingdom of God into our neighborhood," may be confusing for some. Let me define what I mean. To join Jesus in extending the Kingdom (or reign) of God into our neighborhood, one must first grasp several theological shifts the Holy Spirit is guiding the Church in North America through in the first half of the 21st century.

In his book: SHIFT: Three Big Moves for The 21st Century Church, my colleague and founder of Pinnacle Leadership Associates, Mark Tidsworth writes: "Due to acculturation, the North American Church has largely forgotten how to travel. A pivotal question for the 21st century North American Church: 'Can God's people remember how to move, how to travel, how to shift and adapt and morph?' There is this thing called gospel, which at its heart, involves change (metanoia)... repent: to think and act differently."[11]

Our Lord is calling the church in North America to make certain shifts and church leaders are finding fresh inspiration and new life as they lead their congregations through these shifts. Understanding and making the following three shifts is helpful for leaders and congregations called to join Jesus in extending God's Kingdom into the neighborhood.

SHIFT #1: THE SHIFT FROM MAINTENANCE TO MISSIONAL.

In the book Missional Church: A Vision For The Sending of the Church in North America, author Darrell Guder writes: "We have begun to see that the church of Jesus Christ, is not the purpose or goal of the gospel, but rather its instrument and witness...This does not mean that the church is not essential to God's work of salvation – it is. But it is essential as God's chosen people who are blessed to be a blessing to the nations."[12]

11   Mark Tidsworth, SHIFT; Three Big Moves For the 21st Century Church (Columbia: Pinnacle Leadership Press, 2015), 43.
12   Darrell Guder. Missional Church: A Vision for the Sending of the Church in North America (Grand Rapids: Eerdmans, 1998), 4.

Guder has helped the Church understand that growing, sustaining and protecting the institutional church has never been the aim of our missionary God. Instead, Guder helps readers to grasp the Church as a tool our Lord uses for the greater goal of growing the Kingdom of God on earth.

Early in the life of the Bridge Presbyterian Church, our leadership team debated whether or not to share the rental space we were using for Sunday worship with a local Cub Scout pack. The conversation was predictable. About half the leaders around the table were eager for our new church to connect with young families, especially those leaders who were scouts themselves.

But the other half of the leadership team took a more pragmatic approach. They asked the questions responsible leaders need to ask: Will the scouts play with and break the expensive new instruments and sound board our band just purchased? What happens if someone gets hurt? Will our insurance cover our liability?

The longer the conversation lasted the less likely I, as moderator, thought we would gain a consensus. What was unfolding before my eyes was a clash between those raised in a church with a maintenance mentality and those who have been gripped with a missional mindset.

After a lot of respectful conversation, one of the elders raised their hand and said: "Wait, our mission is to be a blessing in this community. We've been called by our Lord to put God's need above our institutional needs. I think the Lord wants us to host the scouts." It didn't take very long after those words were uttered for the elders to approve letting the scouts use our rental facilities. As I write this chapter, some six years after that vote, the scout troop consists of more than 50 cub scouts who (along with their families) fill up our rental facilities every Monday (and nothing has been broken...yet!)

To make the shift from maintenance to missional, we need to

understand what a maintenance mentality looks like in a church and what a missional mindset sounds like when it is embraced by a congregation. Here are some characteristics of a Maintenance-Mentality Church.

Maintenance-Mentality Churches
- Emphasis is on maintaining a tradition or franchising a denomination.
- Emphasis is on being a vendor of religious goods and services in order to meet church consumer's needs.
- Mission is one aspect of the total life of the new church.
- Participants of the new church are thought of as members.
- The mission field is far away.
- God is a personal God.

Now compare the characteristics of a maintenance mentality church with a church that has been gripped by a missional mindset.

Missional-Type New Churches
- Emphasis is on participating in God's mission for the world.
- Emphasis is on calling, equipping and sending believers into the world.
- Mission is central to everything in the new church.
- Participants of the church understand themselves as missionaries.
- The mission field begins at the doorsteps of the church.
- God is a missionary God.[13]

At the Bridge Presbyterian Church, we help those ready to join our new church understand the shift from maintenance to missional by

---

13   Doug Cushing, *Where There's No Road at All: Adventures in Church Planting* (Columbia: Pinnacle Leadership Press, 2013), 16.

using the chart below. By using this chart, we hope that the Holy Spirit grips those who join our new church with a missional mindset.

Church Maintenance Culture	Missional Culture
I'm a member of this church	I'm a partner in God's mission
Membership is something I choose	Covenant Partner is something I am
Membership implies obligations	Covenant Partner implies calling
Membership focus=meeting needs	Covenant Partnership focus=sustaining relationships
What am I entitled to?	What am I responsible for?
What do I get?	How can I give?
What's best for the organization?	What's best for God's Kingdom?

In order for churches and church leaders to understand what it means to "Join Jesus in extending the Kingdom of God into our neighborhood," they must understand and embrace the shift from Maintenance-Mentality to a Missional-Mindset. To better help make this shift, here are some discussion questions for your congregation:

Discussion Questions:

1. Which characteristics of a maintenance-mentality church does your congregation possess?

2. Which characteristics of a missional mindset church does your congregation embrace?

3. What 'one thing' can you do to help your congregation through the shift from maintenance to missional church?

4. How does this passage from John's gospel help you make the shift from maintenance to missional church? "You did not choose me. I choose you...that you should bear fruit." (John 15:16)

5. How does this quote inspire your congregation to make the shift from maintenance to missional? "We find after years of struggle that we do not take a trip; a trip takes us." John Steinbeck

SHIFT #2: THE SHIFT FROM PLACE TO PEOPLE

The second shift congregations need to embrace in order to "Join Jesus in extending the Kingdom of God into our neighborhood," is the shift from understanding the Church as a place to an understanding of the Church as God's people.

When I first arrived in Leland, NC to begin my work of launching what is now the Bridge Presbyterian Church, I did what most church planters do. I gathered a core group of interested seekers. At one of our first gatherings, I asked those in attendance what they were looking for in a new church.

A surprising number of responses were similar. "I want to go to church in Leland with my neighbors instead of going to church across the Bridge in Wilmington," is what I heard. I told this group of folks eager to launch the new church that I was convinced our Lord's goal for the new church was slightly different than what they had just expressed. I told the folks gathered that instead of going to church with our neighbors, our Lord is calling our new church to <u>be</u> the church <u>to</u> our neighbors.

This second shift our Lord is leading within His church requires those who lead and those who faithfully worship and serve to fundamentally change the way they think about church. The Lord is calling His Church to move from the idea of the church as a place to the notion of the church as God's people.

Let's try something: If a new resident in your neighborhood were to ask people in your congregation: "Where is your church?" How would they respond? They would probably reply by pointing the curious new neighbor to <u>where</u> your church is located. They might say something like: "Oh, we are the church at Fourth and Walnut."

Or, consider this: It's 9:30am on a given Sunday. Someone in your congregation is pulling out of their driveway to go to worship. Suddenly, their new neighbor asks them where they were going? How do you think they would reply? They would, likely, say: "I'm going to church." Similarly, if you left your umbrella at the place you regularly attend Sunday worship and your spouse asked you where that red umbrella was, you'd probably tell your spouse: "I left it at church."

In each of those examples, the church is understood as, what? It's understood as a place! The widely held assumption by most Christians is that the church is a place where things happen.[14] But the church is not a place where things happen, is it? Take for example the first storefront where the church I currently serve gathered for Sunday worship in 2014.

Just prior to the Bridge Presbyterian Church renting that place for worship, that place was a storefront that was used to sell used furniture. In 2018, we moved from that storefront into larger, more spacious rental space. The original storefront we used for worship was quickly leased to a different tenant who used that space to sell second-hand furniture.

After four additional years in a larger rental space, the Bridge Presbyterian Church purchased a building and property that we will move into in the fall of 2022. As we prepare to move into our new facility, we do so with the realization that the Church is not, nor ever will be a place. Instead, we've learned that the Church is God's people called and sent on mission.

Because the Church is not a place, but people, God's people must recover their fundamental vocation as being a picture of the risen Lord in real-time to our neighbors. Christians have used a fancy word to describe this belief. It's called being Incarnational. Being Incarnational means "taking on flesh or becoming like someone."[15] At the very beginning of John's gospel, the author was trying to convey that Jesus was the incarnation of God.

In verse 1 we read: "In the beginning was the Word (meaning Jesus). The word was with God and the word was God," (NRSV). Then in verse 14 in the Message translation we read: "The word (meaning Jesus) became flesh and blood, and moved into the neighborhood. We saw the glory with our own eyes, the one-of-a-kind glory, like father, like son, generous inside and out, true from start to finish."

The author of John's gospel wanted his readers to understand that Jesus was a fully-human and fully-divine picture of God in real-time.

---

14   Guder, *Missional Church*, 79.
15   Halter and Smay, *The Tangible Kingdom*, 26.

Have you have seen the Steven Spielberg movie: <u>Lincoln</u>? If so, you were probably as amazed as I was at how closely Daniel Day Lewis resembled our 16[th,] President. There were times during that movie I felt I was looking at a perfect replica of President Lincoln. That wasn't by accident.

In an interview Steven Spielberg gave to Deadline Hollywood, the Academy-Award winning Director revealed that it took nearly 6 years to convince actor Daniel Day-Lewis to play the part of Lincoln. One reason Daniel Day-Lewis repeatedly refused the role of Lincoln was because of how intimidated he felt about playing a larger-than-life figure like Lincoln.

But Spielberg felt like he couldn't make the movie without Daniel Day-Lewis. As Spielberg put it: "I couldn't see Lincoln beyond what I knew Daniel would bring to it; which was going to be an out-of-body experience that would put us in a real-time encounter with the man, his legacy, and that century."[16]

God's will is for everyone to have a real-time encounter with Jesus Christ through the power of the Holy Spirit. After Jesus' death and resurrection, the early Christians knew that it was their responsibility to be Incarnational – to be a picture of the risen Lord in real-time.

The second shift churches and church leaders must make in order to join Jesus in extending his Kingdom in the neighborhood, is the shift from the commonly held understanding of the Church as a place to a missional affirmation of the Church as God's people. As God's people learn to be incarnational, their witness to our risen and reigning Lord in real-time will bless and impact their neighborhoods and their city.

Below you will find some study questions that may help you and your congregation envision the shift from the notion of the Church as a place to idea of the Church as God's people.

16   Jordan Zakarin, "Steven Spielberg Reveals Daniel Day Lewis Original 'Lincoln' Rejection Letter," *The Hollywood Reporter*, January 8, 2013, https://www.hollywoodreporter.com/news/general-news/steven-spielberg-reveals-daniel-day-409709/ .

Discussion Questions:

1. Do the people associated with your congregation understand 'Church' more as a place or a people?

2. How would explain 'being Incarnational' to your leadership team?

3. Discuss one or two ways you can help lead the shift in understanding from a church as a place to a church as people sent on mission with God?

4. What are some ways your congregation is currently being a blessing – the tangible touch of God to their neighbors?

5. Discuss how this passage of Scripture informs your understanding of being incarnational?_ "The Word became flesh and blood and moved into the neighborhood." (John 1:14)

6. How does this quote help explain what it means for the church to bear witness to Jesus in the world? "We are called to be Jesus in real-time to our neighbors."

SHIFT #3: FROM SENDING TO BEING SENT

A third shift churches and church leaders must make in order to join Jesus in extending his Kingdom in your neighborhood is the shift in thinking from the notion of sending others on mission work to the new reality that every Christian is sent. The Spirit is calling the Church to change the way it understands mission from the idea of sending others to the notion of being sent.

If you grew up in the church, you likely understood a missionary as someone of uncommon faith and courage. A missionary was someone whose faith led them to accept God's call to go to some remote corner of the world and serve the Church as a missionary. So, a missionary was a technical title given to someone who received cross-cultural training and was then sent by the Church (usually over some large body of water) to some primitive outpost.

Consequently, the notion that every Christian is sent by God can feel overwhelming, even threatening to most Christians. The theological affirmation that every Christian is sent subverts the mindset, so prevalent in the previous century, that only extraordinary Christians are sent by God to do mission work.

So, while this theological shift may feel threatening, it need not. When we, at the Bridge Presbyterian Church discussed how we can embody this shift from sending to being sent, we did so by inviting everyone at the Bridge to develop a very simple, yet effective habit of being a blessing – the tangible touch of God to people in their neighborhoods.

This language is borrowed from an important book written by Hugh Halter and Matt Smay titled: The Tangible Kingdom. What's really cool about this habit is that being a blessing is non-threatening. Not everyone is up to the lofty theological affirmation that they are sent by God. But everyone can envision some way they can be a blessing – the tangible touch of God to their neighbors. Everyone can do that...and everyone can do it well.

The 12th chapter of Genesis helps us think about how to bless others. Genesis 12 is the story of God calling Abraham and Sarah. Some scholars refer to this story as the lynchpin of the entire Bible. Yeah... it's that important to overall biblical narrative of God's saving, healing and redeeming the world.

At the center of the story, we meet an aging couple, Abraham and Sarah, two of the most unlikely people to be used by God. Yet, God called them to leave their country, most of their family and all the security of home in order to go to a strange and far away land.

In chapter 12, beginning at verse one, we read: "Now the Lord said to Abram, "Go from your country and your kindred and your father's house to the land that I will show you. I will make of you a great nation, and I will bless you, and make your name great, so that you will be a blessing." Then in verse 4 we read: "So Abraham went."

While reading the book Tangible Kingdom, I stumbled across this important insight. The authors write: "God didn't call Abraham (and Sarah) or the early communities (of Christians) to be evangelistic, share four laws, or hand out tracts. God told them to bless the world with the blessing God gave them. Blessing means 'the tangible touch of God.'" [17]

Did you catch that? God sent Abraham and Sarah to be God's first missionaries with one simple command: be a blessing! God didn't tell the couple to convert the natives or build a mission hospital. God didn't demand they do street evangelism or build a huge new church.

God gave them a simple command. God said: "Be a blessing!" You know what God did NOT say to Abraham and Sarah? God did NOT say: "Be a blessing...one day a week." God's plan to turn the world back to God required Abraham and Sarah to bless others daily.

Let's linger on this point for a second: Abraham and Sarah didn't

17   Halter and Smay, *Tangible Kingdom*, 11.

have the luxury of gathering weekly with a group of like-minded individuals in a fancy storefront to worship God, drink some coffee and listen to some awesome praise music. Nor did the couple have the opportunity to work at the local Christian radio station or volunteer at the local food pantry.

They lived out their calling by being a blessing to others every day. They didn't silo their creative passion to bless the world into a single day of the week. Abraham and Sarah changed the world by blessing others every day.

Not everyone is called to be an evangelist. Not everyone is called to be a pastor or an elder or a seminary professor. But everyone...every single one of us can be a blessing to our friends; to our neighbors; to our co-workers; to the woman at the coffee shop and to the guy who bags our groceries. With prayer and creativity every single one of us can be a blessing every single day, right?

Please use the questions below to engage your congregation or leadership team in a discussion about making the shift from sending to being sent.

Discussion Questions:

1. Do a quick audit and share one way your congregation is learning to send its people into the neighborhood to be a blessing and one way it is not doing so.

2. How could you lead your congregation in making the shift from not merely telling people about Jesus to being a blessing – the tangible touch of God?

3. Discuss this verse and the larger passage with your group. What did God mean when God called Abraham and Sarah to be a blessing? "So that you will be a blessing." (Gen 10:4)

At the Bridge Presbyterian Church we are learning to make these theological shifts in our thinking. Faithful to the leading of our Lord, we are going about making the shift from a maintenance-minded to a missional-minded congregation. We are recovering God's vision for the Church as God's people not as a place and we are, increasingly, submitting ourselves to God's calling and sending us to be a blessing – the tangible touch of God in our neighborhoods.

The ultimate goal of making these shifts is to better enable us to join Jesus in extending the Kingdom of God to our neighborhood. We believe that the innovative ways our missional sermon-based small groups integrate; Sunday worship; fellowship; prayer; Christian formation and mission help us encounter the Holy Spirit and equip us to join Jesus in mission.

In chapter two, I will share my vision for a missional sermon-based small group ministry at the Bridge; discuss the benefits of this kind of small group and lay out a process for you to launch missional sermon-based small groups in your church. Chapter three will be a short chapter discussing the art of asking questions in worship and how asking questions in worship fosters the growth of missional sermon-based small groups.

Chapter four will provide examples of sermons and small group study guides. Chapter five will discuss how to tie missional small groups into the larger vision and mission of your congregation. I will also provide an appendix with helpful tools you can use or adapt to help your efforts to begin missional sermon-based small groups in your church.

In their book: <u>And: The Gathered and Scattered Church</u>, the authors express the feeling of so many dedicated disciples who faithfully worship and serve their Lord and his Church. Do these words get your pulse racing?

"I believe that God's people want to go BIG! They're tired of being the unsent church-weary of church services, sermons, in-house programs, and Bible studies that never push them out and challenge them to really be the missional people God has called them to be." What follows is my description of a church-wide system designed to challenge God's people to really be the missional people God has called them to be. If that is what you long for, I encourage you to read on![18]

---

18   Hugh Halter and Matt Smay, *And: The Gathered and Scattered Church* (Grand Rapids: Zondervan, 2010), 48.

CHAPTER TWO

MAKING THE SHIFT TO MISSIONAL SERMON-BASED SMALL GROUPS

THE ROLE OF A SMALL GROUP TEAM

Are you feeling the nudge of the Holy Spirit to make the shift to a missional sermon-based small group ministry within your congregation? Perhaps it's more than a nudge? Maybe, you sense how this sort of small group ministry could change everything within your congregation? Perhaps, you've caught a glimpse of how this type of small group ministry could revive the weary, post-pandemic spirit of your congregation while also renewing your passion for parish ministry?

If that is you, then you are ready to take make the shift but you are wondering how to begin the conversation about missional sermon-based small groups within your leadership team and/or your congregation?

The first and most important step is to pray and follow the lead of the Holy Spirit. In her book titled: Sailboat Church, author Joan Gray discusses the difference between Rowboat churches – those congregations that try to do everything under their own power verse Sailboat churches – those congregations that are able to catch the wind of the Holy Spirit and let that wind guide their life. Gray points out how Sailboat churches live between two powerful realities:

"Without me you can do nothing," (John 15:5, NRSV)
"With God nothing is impossible," (Luke 1: 35-37, NRSV)

Gray writes: "The bedrock reality of life in the Sailboat church is that God 'through the power at work within us can do abundantly far more than we could ever ask or imagine,' (Eph. 3:21). Sailboat churches tend to focus not on their own situation, resources, or limitation but rather on discerning God's unfolding will...these congregations live in the creative tension between two spiritual realities. The first of these realities we hear from Jesus at the Last Supper with his disciples: 'Without me you can do nothing,' (John 15:5, NRSV)."[19]

Gray's point is that without Jesus in the center of congregational life, it is impossible to accomplish our Lord's mission. While we know this to be true, deep down we still feel that it's all up to us. So, we row as hard as we can, thinking that a new ministry or program is our responsibility. However, Sailboat churches realize that they can tap into spiritual resources beyond themselves by reorienting their efforts and catching the wind of the Spirit.

Gray continues: "The second reality in Sailboat churches live by is heard in the angel Gabriel's response to Mary's question: 'I am a virgin. How can I bear a child?' Gabriel's response is elegantly simple: 'With God nothing is impossible,' (Luke 1:35-37, NRSV)."[20]

Only congregations that are living into a transforming relationship with this God for whom nothing is impossible can hope to successfully launch missional sermon-based small groups. If prayer and discernment of the Spirit are step 1a and 1b, then getting other leaders and lay people involved is step 2.

Every congregation has a leadership structure. We Presbyterians elect elders to serve on a governing board referred to as a Session. The Session of most Presbyterian Churches looks and acts remarkably similar to leadership teams in other denominations. Like your congregation, we have an Elder (leader) who oversees worship and an Elder who oversee

19   Joan Gray, *Sailboat Church: Helping Your Church Rethink Its Mission and Practice* (Louisville: Westminster John Knox Press, 2014), 4-8.
20   John Gray, *Sailboat Church*, p 4 – 8.

finances and an elder who oversees Christian Education – along with teams of people who are called to work collaboratively with each Elder.

At the Bridge, we created a position called Small Group elder who oversees all small group activities. This elder along with a team of small group leaders form our small group team. Together they meet to plan, resource and review all small group activities within our congregation (missional sermon-based small groups are not the only small groups at the Bridge).

A wise and effective starting point for launching missional sermon-based small groups in your congregation would be to identify a lay leader to serve as the leader of small groups – just as we elected a Small Group elder to oversee our small groups. Then, gather interested and called volunteers to join the team.

Alternatively, some congregations have created a paid staff position to oversee the entire small group ministry of the church. The job description for the elder of Small Groups at the Bridge looks like this:

MISSIONAL SERMON-BASED SMALL GROUP LEADER JOB DESCRIPTION

Small Group Leader/Elder Overview (John 1: 46, NRSV)

- People who are searching for significant relationships and safe places to explore their faith journey need a place where they feel they belong.
- People need to feel they belong before they will become a part of a church or believe the church's teachings.
- At the Bridge, seekers will discover a sense of belonging in small groups.

How will our church oversee missional sermon-based small groups?

The Small Group Team will be a standing ministry team of the Session, led by an elder. The Team will:

Grow & Develop Sermon-Based Small Groups –

- The team will ensure Sermon-Based Small Groups are resourced, facilitated and led by trained people.
- The team will make sure everyone interested is assimilated into a small group.
- The team will publicize small group offerings in the congregation.
- The team will provide training for leaders and develop a yearly calendar.

Grow & Develop Other Small Groups –

- The team will help cast a vision that small groups are central to what we do at the Bridge.
- The team will help develop other types of small groups including a) affinity groups ie: hiking small group; cooking small group; b) service groups ie: Matthew's Ministry team; Harbor House team

What will missional sermon-based small groups look like?

- Participants will actively participate in weekly small groups.
- Sermon-based small groups and other small groups will have a staff person and a ministry team of session that resources the program.
- Twice yearly leadership training will take place for SBSG leaders.

How does this core habit connect to our mission statement?

- This core habit will help people connect with 'God's passion, people and purpose for life.[21]

- *"Instead of doing groups for the sake of experiencing community, groups experience community for the sake of participating in God's redemption of creation."*

How do we know we are faithful to this core habit?

- The metrics used to evaluate how this team is cultivating the core habit of belonging in small groups include: 1) This core habit will be evaluated twice annually in terms of percentage of participants involved in small groups. 2) Tracking the percentage of participants in quarterly mission projects.

As you read this job description you need to understand that at the Bridge, each of our elder job descriptions has to tie into one of our eight church-wide core habits and must answer the questions:

- How do we oversee this core habit?
- How do we live into this core habit?
- How does the core habit connect to our mission statement?
- How do we know we are faithful to this core habit?

However, establishing a leadership position within your congregation dedicated to overseeing all small group activity may be too big of a leap for your congregation – even if the pandemic has stirred a restlessness within your congregation and they are eager to innovate. In some congregations, making such a decisive shift may be met with resistance and, in some instances, sabotage.

Resistance within a church system is typically a sign that things are moving too quickly. In their insightful book: <u>Thriving Through Ministry Conflict By Understanding Your Red and Blue Zones,</u> the authors James

---

21   At the Bridge Presbyterian Church we align our small group ministry with our core habits and our mission statement. See chapter 5 for a detailed description.

Osterhaus, Joseph Jerkowski and Todd Hahn point out that: "resistance is your ally. It's your ally not your enemy, because it shows you that what you are doing is not working...in fact, it can be the best teacher you have ever had."[22] So, it may be unwise for a pastor or church officer to move too quickly in identifying a leader of the small group ministry or forming a team of dedicated volunteers to overseeing that ministry.[23]

If you feel that missional sermon-based small groups may be where the Spirit is leading your congregation, but you believe that the wisest course of action is to proceed gradually, then I suggest a simpler and more basic step be to gather a Circle Of Ten. The Circle of Ten is a group of lay people who are called and committed to help birth a missional sermon-based small group ministry in your congregation and follow my recommendations below for a pilot project.

DEVELOPING A MISSIONAL SERMON-BASED SMALL GROUP PILOT PROJECT

There is no magic behind the number ten. In some congregations it may be easy to raise up ten interested folks while in other congregations four to six ministry partners may be more realistic. I chose ten because that would be an ideal size for the missional sermon-based small group pilot project I will describe below. Additionally, ten people will provide ample number of volunteers to help with the nuts and bolts to successfully get this ministry off the ground in your church. Here are a few tips for gathering your Circle Of Ten.

PREPARING YOUR PILOT PROJECT: GATHING YOUR CIRCLE OF TEN

22   James Osterhaus, Joseph M. Jurkowski and Todd A. Hahn, *Thriving Through Ministry Conflict by Understanding Your Red and Blue Zones* (Grand Rapids: Zondervan, 2005), pg location 792.
23   See an important discussion about leadership and sabotage in Tod Bolsinger, *Tempered Resilience: How Leaders Are Formed in the Crucible of Change* (Downer's Grove: Intervarsity Press, 2022), p 22ff.

1. <u>Pray, trusting the Holy Spirit is already at work</u> – I was committed to making the Bridge a church of small groups rather than a church with small groups.[24] But I had never organized a congregation around small groups. Believing that organizing a church of small groups was part of the Lord's vision for the Bridge Presbyterian Church, I began to pray, asking the Lord to lead me. Although I shouldn't have been surprised, I was shocked to discover how many of the new people God was sending to our new church had experience in small groups. You may be surprised to discover how the Lord has been preparing you to uncover your <u>Circle Of Ten</u>.

2. <u>Identify people you think are ready and eager to make the shift</u> – You likely already know a number of people who are hungry for new ways to study God's Word in small groups. You probably can identify people in your congregation who yearn to join a group where they can pray, study and be on mission, together. Meet with those people one on one and cast the vision for missional sermon-based small groups. Listen to their objections, concerns and affirmations.

3. <u>Invite those who express interest in missional sermon-based small groups to meet as a small group</u> – Whether you have ten interested people ready to gather or not, gather the growing group of interested folks and begin discussing the vision for missional sermon-based small groups, together. Structure your time together in a way that replicates the structure of the missional sermon-based small groups that I will outline below. Alternatively, you and your <u>Circle of Ten</u> can study this book, together.

4. <u>Decision time</u> – In most congregations it is wise to inform

---

24   I understand the distinction between a church 'of' small group and a church 'with' small groups this way. If a congregation has, at least, 50% of its members actively involved in a small group then it is a church 'of' small groups.

the leadership team of the work you are doing to form your Circle Of Ten as soon as it is prudently possible. Sometimes it is prudent to inform the leadership of the church about your intention at the very beginning of the process. Other times, it is wise to do the preliminary work of identifying your Circle of Ten; gauging interest and commitment and listening to lay people provide wisdom and advise and then present your vision to the leadership team. Either way, honest, transparent communication with your church's leadership team (early on) is essential.

5. Launch Time – After you have gathered your Circle Of Ten, cast the vision and gained support of your church leadership team, it's time to launch a missional sermon-based small group pilot project. Begin by creating a plan for explaining to the congregation in advance what you intend to launch; why you intend to launch a mission sermon-based small groups; when it will happen and how the sermon-based small groups will impact worship. If possible, members of your Circle Of Ten should be intimately involved in deciding what to say to the congregation as well as sharing the excitement of the upcoming pilot project during worship.

6. Create Publicity for The Upcoming Sermon-Series – One way to create interest in your missional sermon-based small group pilot project is to create some buzz around the upcoming sermon series. Whether you are a lectionary-based preacher or someone who is comfortable preaching a sermon series, publicize the upcoming sermon series in your e-newsletter, social media and from the pulpit. The goal is to inform and to create curiosity among the congregation. If launching a pilot project will be received by some as a threat or an unwelcome change, then

make sure to create an avenue for folks to ask questions and receive responses prior to launch.

7. Continue meeting with Circle Of Ten – As you prepare for the launching of the pilot program, meet a few more times with the Circle Of Ten. The most important activity you can do, together, is pray. Praying for the pilot program not only allows the wind of the Spirit to guide your actions, it also binds the Circle Of Ten together. I would also encourage you to use this book as a resource for helping to cast a vision with your Circle of Ten. Additionally, you will want to explain to the Circle Of Ten the flow and structure of the weekly small groups; how to integrate worship and small group life; how to discern a mission project together and finally, to provide them with a small group covenant to discuss and agree upon. You will find a) missional small group guide for leaders and facilitators; b) an FAQ document for small groups; c) a sample sign-up sheet for small groups; d) an example of a missional sermon-based small group study guide in the appendix. Alternatively, you can lead the Circle of Ten through this book, paying special attention to the study questions embedded in each section.

8. Launch Pilot Project – Dedicate the ten in worship with a prayer and have them be prepared to report back to the congregation at the end of the small group. You could even craft an entire worship service around small groups that includes time for the Circle of Ten to share their experience and then to commission the group to do the work of forming a small group ministry within your congregation.

Discussion Questions:

Here are a few questions to discuss during the initial gathering with folks interested in developing a small group ministry within your congregation.

1. What is the Spirit saying to you about small groups?

2. How will missional sermon-based small groups help fulfill our larger mission in the community around our congregation?

3. What kind of sermon series might the Spirit be calling us to create that would be a blessing to the congregation while also inspiring them to be a blessing; the tangible touch of God in the neighborhoods around our church?

4. Who else might be interested in joining this conversation?

5. How might the information you have read so far help cast a vision for small groups in our congregation?

6. When should we begin? Who will facilitate our first small group series? Where will it be held?

7. How will we talk about this vision for missional sermon-based

small groups with our leadership and our congregation? How will we report back to the congregation about our experience in a missional sermon-based small group?

THE ROLE OF THE PASTOR

Obviously, the role of the Pastor is central to a successful missional sermon-based small group program. The primary component of the small-groups is the weekly sermon. As I mentioned earlier, you can develop a thriving missional sermon-based small group ministry whether you are a lectionary-based preacher or one who is familiar with preaching sermons that are structured into a six-to-ten-week series. The keys to effective sermon writing for small groups are:

1. Make sure your sermons are rooted in God's Word – I typically use an Old Testament, New Testament and epistle passage. If you are like me, you probably want to explore all the passages you cite in detail throughout the sermon, but usually focus on one passage more than the others. If your sermons typically emphasize one of the selected passages of Scripture more than the others, then the missional sermon-based study guide becomes the perfect vehicle for you to focus on the other passages you used in the sermon. Additionally, it will allow the small group participants the option of drilling down on passages you have only touched on in the sermon.

2. Make sure your sermons contain illustrations and quotes – Illustrations and quotes are often the way listeners 'get it.' Using illustrations and quotes, and then referring to them in the study guide questions is not only a wonderful teaching tool, it also keeps the level of engagement high in worship and during the

small group. As a Presbyterian, dropping quotes by Karl Barth in a sermon can be a little overwhelming for listeners. But putting the same Barth quote into a question within the study guide, allows for folks to dissect the quote and discuss it.

3. Create sermons that use questions – Perhaps nothing is more important to crafting sermons for small groups than learning how to incorporate questions in the homiletical task. I've dedicated the next chapter to a brief description of how to develop the art of asking questions in worship

Crafting sermons for missional sermon-based small groups carries with it a big challenge and an even bigger pay-off. Finding this new rhythm will take a while, and it will be a challenge. But, in time, you will certainly celebrate the pay-off.

The Big Challenge – I have found that I am most comfortable preparing and launching a new round of small groups when I have written the entire series of sermons in advance. Yes, I said - the ENTIRE series of sermons. This is not essential for an effective missional sermon-based small group ministry and it may be overwhelming to even consider. But this sort of preparation has a number of advantages. Most importantly, having the entire series of sermons written in advance allows you, as worship leader and preacher, to have a full grasp on the direction and major points to emphasize during the series.

Additionally, having the entire series of sermons written (or at least outlined) in advance provides participants with the clear understanding of how long the series will last. Moreover, having the entire series of sermons written in advance will help you when you meet with the facilitators to discuss the flow and direction of the series and what points the facilitators should emphasize.

Another benefit to writing the series of sermons in advance is that the leaders will provide you with feedback – letting you know what participants are not understanding; what participants feel you are repeating; what participants feel is not being addressed. This allows you to tweak future sermons in the series, if needed.

Finally, having the entire series of sermons written in advance (while it will require some long evenings and/or weekends of preparation) will allow you time in advance to begin creatively planning for the next series of sermons. If you are like me, creativity happens when I'm not rushed.

The Big Pay-Off – The biggest pay-off of writing your four-to-eight-week sermon series in advance is simple. The sermons are DONE! If you choose to write the sermons in advance, I would suggest that the pilot program last four to six weeks.

A TYPICAL MISSIONAL SERMON-BASED SMALL GROUP SERIES: THE NUTS AND BOLTS

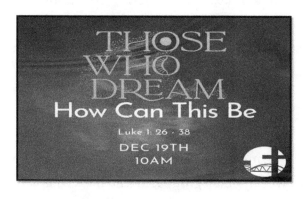

At the church I serve, we typically run missional sermon-based small groups quarterly. Our missional sermon-based small groups usually last 6 – 10 weeks depending upon the season of the year; the particular series and my level of inspiration. For example, our congregation celebrates the seasons of Advent and Lent. Typically, my sermon series in the season of Advent is 4 -5 weeks long corresponding with the four Sundays of Lent and Christmas Eve.

That said, the sermon series for Advent 2021 was titled: Those Who

Dream.[25] The series of sermons I was led to craft stretched past Christmas Eve and ended on Epiphany Sunday. During the 2021 Lenten season, I preached a series of sermons titled: The Gospel of Mark: Unanticipated Good News. The series continued beyond the Lenten season into the season of Eastertide.

However, and this is important to note, occasionally I will create a sermon series that will last longer than the small group wants to meet.

I've discovered that the ideal length for missional sermon-based small groups is four to eight weeks in length. Less than four weeks does not allow a full immersion into the sermon theme. After eight weeks, the small groups typically feel saturated with the theme.

Once the small group has completed the series, they typically take a break and then regroup for the next sermon series. At the Bridge, I typically offer 4 sermon series per year. Some groups stay together throughout the year and study the sermons that are preached between sermon series.

THE ROLE OF THE FACILITATORS

The primary role of the missional sermon-based small group facilitators is to convene the weekly small group and lead the discussion. While it is not always doable, we have discovered that co-facilitators work best for missional sermon-based small groups. The reasons are fairly straightforward.

---

25   Those Who Dream was a series that I stumbled into as I browsed through an online resource called Sanctified Art. I highly recommend the work of those creative souls who create amazing resources for congregations and pastors. Check out their website at: https:// sanctifiedart.org/

1. <u>Co-facilitators makes it easier to recruit small group leaders</u> - Perhaps the number one reason why people decline to be facilitators is because they know they have a commitment ie; travel, family event that prevents them from committing to four to eight straight weeks of facilitating the small group.

2. <u>Co-facilitators allows for a more equal distribution of the tasks of leading a small group</u> - One facilitator typically will lead the discussion while the other facilitator will organize prayer concerns and help spearhead the mission project.

3. <u>Co-facilitators work together to problem solve and care for their group</u> - A number of the challenges that facilitators face include: a) there may be a few voices that dominate the small group; b) there may be a few voices that bring their political or theological agenda to the discussion and intentionally or unintentionally cause the small group to veer off topic; c) there may be a conflict between two or more participants. Co-facilitators can pray together, problem-solve together and jointly discuss any challenges that arise during the small group series.

Before each round of missional sermon-based small groups, our small group elder and I meet with the facilitators for a training. During the training I try to discuss the focus and flow of the upcoming series. See Appendix for training materials.

Concurrently, we begin the publicity for the new round of missional sermon-based small groups. The word publicity has negative connotations in religious circles. I get that. But, as you grow and develop your missional sermon-based small group ministry, you'll learn that the congregation wants to know, in advance, when the next series will begin and what it's about. Additionally, they will want time to sign-up for the small groups. Publicizing the new series, a month or so in advance will help alleviate those concerns.

Early on, we encouraged small groups to stay together for an entire calendar year and then, if the participants want to relocate to a different small group, they are free to do so at the beginning of the new year. However, we found that most participants want the freedom to stay with their small group, drop out or change to a different small group. So, we while we encourage small groups to stay together for a calendar year, we don't make that a mandatory requirement.

Additionally, publicity creates some buzz around the upcoming series. It allows you to challenge the congregation; perk their interest; speak to those yet to join a small group and draw newer visitors into small groups.

We typically begin publicizing and asking folks to sign-up about a month prior to the launching of the new series. Prior to the publicity launch, our small group elder has already identified the facilitator or co-facilitators as well as the day, time and location of the small group.

Sign-up sheets are available online and are also in the foyer so folks can sign-up before and after worship. The sign-up sheets typically include the sermon series icon; the facilitators names; the location; day and time of the study.

While most conventional material on how to grow a small group ministry emphasizes the importance of meeting in homes, we've discovered that it's easier to secure facilitators if we offer the option of meeting in their home or at the Bridge facility. We've learned that some people are willing to facilitate a small group but want nothing to do with getting their home 'small-group-ready,' every week.

So, while I agree that meeting in a home is preferable to meeting at a room in the church facility or on-campus, I let the facilitators decide when and where they want to meet. Additionally, there has been one small group that meets immediately after Sunday worship at the Bridge

Presbyterian Church. While I prefer to spread out the small group meetings during the week, I realize that there are a group of people who are eager to meet and discuss immediately after worship. I have included a sample of a missional sermon-based small group sign-up sheet in the appendix.

Additionally, we begin publicizing the series in our e-newsletter, on social media platforms and in the pulpit. I create a sermon series graphic and short write up about the series. Writing the brief description of the series, I try to appeal to people within our congregation as well as people who may see the publicity on-line. As you might guess, getting the sermon series publicity onto social media in advance is a great way to connect with people who may be looking for a church home.

Here is an example of a recent missional sermon-based small group sermon icon and the description of the series we used for our publicity.

Our next sermon series is titled: The Story of Naaman: Finding Healing From our Fatal Flaws. In the series, we will be introduced to a Syrian army General named Naaman who was obsessed with finding healing from a lethal skin disease called Leprosy. What Naaman didn't realize was that his real problem was more than skin deep. His real problem was sin.

Like Naaman we all have our flaws that, if we are not careful, can be fatal. Those flaws are called sin. It's only after we acknowledge our sin (our fatal flaws) that we can begin the process of healing. If you've ever driven a car that is out of alignment you know how easily you can end up in a ditch on the side of the road.

Sin is our, human, alignment problem. Sin is the force within our lives that will always lead us into the ditch. But here is the really good news. Admitting we have this leprosy called sin is an admission of hope – hope that things might change. Naaman's path toward healing started once he acknowledged his problem and decided he needed to do something about it.

As I mentioned earlier, I write my sermons ahead of time so that they are done prior to launching the series. However, my rhythm has been to write the missional sermon-based small group study guide the week prior to the sermon being preached. So, if week three of the series begins with the sermon on Sunday May 8th, I will write the study guide for week three early during the week of May 1 – 7. I will then email the completed study guide, along with a hard copy of the sermon, to the facilitators on the Thursday prior (Thursday May 5th in the example above).

The Story of Naaman: Week III
Monday May 1 – Begin writing Week III Study Guide
Thursday May 5 – Send Week III Study Guide/Sermon Hard Copy to facilitators. Facilitators send study guide to small group.
Sunday May 8 – Preach Week III Sermon

The facilitators will then email the study guide alone to the participants. Putting the study guide into the hands of the participants carries with it a number of advantages. Participants can look over the study guide in advance of Sunday worship, allowing them to be better prepared for the hearing and responding to God's Word. The participants can choose to print a copy of the study guide and bring it with them to worship. Those who are unable to attend in-person are able to use the study guide to as part of their virtual worship.

After Sunday worship (and only after worship) are the facilitators allowed to send a sermon copy to all participants. If the copy goes out before the sermon is preached its kind of like cheating for the participants and the miracle of hearing and responding to the word proclaimed is somehow diminished. That said, I realize that some folks will be unable to attend worship in-person or virtually but still want to participate in their small group. Providing a sermon copy after the completion of worship allows congregants who are traveling or tied up to stay connected to their small group and prepared for the discussion.

HOW TO CRAFT A MISSIONAL SERMON-BASED SMALL GROUP STUDY GUIDE

We structure our small groups around our church mission statement.

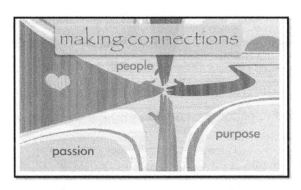

Our mission statement at the Bridge is to help seekers connect with God's people, God's passion and God's purpose for life. Our small groups move seamlessly through three segments that help participants grow deeper in the three connections highlighted in our mission statement:

Connect with God's people –

- (15 minutes) This is typically social time where folks get caught up with each other, informally share their lives. We encourage beverages, snacks, informal chatter during this time. The goal, of course, is to foster a deeper connection with each other and create a community where Jesus is central. Typically, one of the facilitators will collect prayer requests and offer prayer. This is the part of the small group where participants are most likely to connect with God's people in their life.

Connect with God's passion/presence –

- (45 minutes) This is typically heart and soul of the study. The biblical texts from the sermon along with quotes and or illustrations from the sermon are studied through carefully crafted questions that the pastor creates. This section concludes with two or three questions for personal application. This section is the part of the study where participants are most likely to connect with God's passionate love for them.

Connect with God's purpose –

- (15 minutes) During the first small group meeting, participants are asked to prayerfully discern where and how they feel the Lord is calling them to join Jesus on mission in the community. Specifically, each group is encouraged to prayerfully collaborate to determine a mission project they feel called to do, together. Alternatively, the group can choose to join Jesus on mission by participating with one of the sustainable mission partners our church has developed.

- If the small group elects to participate with one of the mission partners of our church, then each small group is required to identity that mission partnership early on; discussing with a representative of that organization how to join them on mission during the sermon series (or shortly after the series) followed by sharing the story of how the group was on mission, together, with the congregation in worship. For example, one missional sermon-based small group might elect to participate in filling backpacks with food for children suffering from food scarcity through our partnership with a local organization Matthew's Ministry. Another small group may elect to spend a Saturday doing yard work and clean up at New Hope Clinic – a non-profit organization dedicated to providing health care for low-income families.

It's important to note that the sub-headings we use to structure our weekly study guide are unique to the Bridge Presbyterian Church. Our language of "connecting with God's purpose, people and passion," is intentional, yet unique to our understanding of our mission. You may choose any sub-heading you wish to structure your weekly study guide. The sub-headings can be as simple as: We Gather; We Study; We Serve.

That said, I would strongly recommend that you use language for the three sub-headings of your study guide that tie into your congregation's mission statement or vision statement. For a fuller discussion of why and how to align your small group ministry with your church mission statement see chapter five.

THE GENIUS OF MISSION SERMON-BASED SMALL GROUPS: INTEGRATION

Way, way back; a long time ago; when I began my ministry career – shortly after the Protestant Reformation (well, it kind of feels that way), the churches I served would uncritically plan occasional all-church events. Maybe the church would plan a *fellowship event* like a church potluck. Perhaps the church would plan a church-wide *mission project* like serving at a local food pantry. Sometimes the church would combine all the Sunday school classes together for an annual Christian Education Kick-Off Sunday.

The assumptions driving those decisions was that there are occasions in the life of a congregation when it is best for the entire Body of Christ to gather together. That assumption is still valid today. However, these all-church occasions were typically stand-alone events that focused exclusively on one aspect of congregational life. These siloed all-church events seldom, if ever, provided the congregation with an integrated vision of what their shared life in Christ might be or what it means to be God's called and sent people in fellowship, worship, mission and study, simultaneously.

The down-side of these siloed, all-church events was that they left congregants confused about the important relationship between koinonia (fellowship) and studying God's Word (Christian formation) or unable to make the connection between God gathering people for worship and then sending people on mission.

I often wondered what it might be like for a church to intentionally integrate fellowship, worship, mission, prayer and Christian formation into a regular rhythm and around a centralized theme. How might things be different if a majority of the members of a particular church were talking about the same things in worship; in Christian education class and during their fellowship, together? How might that impact a congregation's understanding of the Church; its mission in the world and it's Lord?

Additionally, how might things change if a church could create a simple and clear path for members to participate in weekly fellowship, Christian formation, worship and mission in a way that was user-friendly and reduced the amount of time people needed to commit to their church? Might there be a way to prevent members from being put in the unenviable position of having to choose between a family function and the Saturday church mission outreach to the local food pantry?

My vision for missional sermon-based small groups integrates worship, mission, fellowship, prayer and Christian formation. People who are fully participating in a yearly rhythm of missional sermon-based small groups will find they are more deeply involved in the church's mission; more deeply connected to members of the congregation; more enthusiastic in their participation in worship while also growing deeper in their love, understanding and devotion to the Lord.

The reasons are easy to understand. First, missional sermon-based small groups create a simple rhythm for members to participate in weekly fellowship, Christian formation; worship and mission in a way that actually reduces the time commitment and increases the joy and wonder of church membership.

Let's imagine that your congregation is about to begin a five-week missional sermon-based small group series for the Advent season titled: Hope, Peace, Joy and Love: The Wonders of Advent! You have four small groups, each consisting of eight to 12 participants including the facilitators. During those traditionally busy weeks leading up to Christmas, all the participants have to do is show up for Sunday worship (60 minutes [or so]); show up for small group (90 minutes) and they will have experienced Koinonia (Christian fellowship); worship and Christian formation twice in one week all for the low, low price of... wait for it – two to three hours. They will only be leaving their home twice in one week.

Week One; The Wonders of Advent
Sunday Worship = 60 minutes (or so)
Small Group = 90 minutes (or so)
TOTAL = 2 – 2.5 hours of commitment per week

Now, let's do the math for the entire five-week series. Your Advent series on The Wonders of Advent has asked small group participants to leave their homes for a church-related event 10 times (five Sunday worship services and five small group gatherings) with a total invest-ment of 10 – 13 hours to the mission and ministry of your church. Additionally, they will have been on mission with their small group for anywhere between 1 – 3 hours depending on the chosen mission project. This brings the grand total to 11 church-related events with a total investment of 11 – 16 hours in one month!

> Five Week Series: The Wonders of Advent
> Five Sunday Worship Services = 5 hours
> Five Weekly Small Group Gatherings = 5 to 8 hours
> One Small Group Mission Project = 1 – 3 hours
> TOTAL 11 Church-Related Events / 11 – 16 hours

In exchange for that modest time commitment, small-group par-ticipants were able to fellowship with other members and friends on ten different occasions (5 times in worship and 5 times in small group). Additionally, participants enjoyed 5 worship services; studied God's Word, together 5 times (ten if you include hearing the sermons in Sun-day worship) and have collaborated and joined together in following Jesus on mission in the neighborhood. And, the participants have all been studying and having conversation and prayer around the same topic.

Do you see why I say that missional sermon-based small groups are more exciting and compelling way to do church? Especially as the pandemic winds down and members are traveling more and or staying home to worship, do you see how this can unite and recharge your congregation?

Not only do missional sermon-based small groups integrate some of the basic needs of church members like fellowship, mission, worship and study into a simple rhythm that increases participation, missional sermon-based small groups also offer added benefits for the participants.

THE BENEFITS OF MISSIONAL SERMON-BASED SMALL GROUPS IN WORSHIP

Missional sermon-based small groups create a symbiosis between worship and small groups. In Sunday worship, I typically project two or three of the small group questions on the screens prior to the reading and proclaiming of God's Word. In chapter three, I will discuss the art of asking questions in worship.

By asking the entire assembled congregation these questions, I am preparing them to hear God's Word and increasing anticipation for the participants to discuss these questions during the week. Additionally, at the conclusion of our small group series, when our small groups share what they have done on mission during worship, the congregation is inspired and bound more deeply together in our shared life.

Sharing what the small groups have done on mission during Sunday worship has a profound impact on visitors. Visitors see and hear how excited the small groups are about how they have joined Jesus on mission in the neighborhood and are often compelled to learn more.

Additionally, participation in missional sermon-based small groups can increase worship attendance. Not only that but participants are more attentive to the Spirit's leading in worship because they know they will be discussing the sermon and Scripture during the week. This, in turn, leads to increased retention of the salient points of the sermon and, most importantly, the passages of Scripture.

It is not uncommon for participants to come to worship with an outline in hand. Having taken notes during the sermon, folks feel as if they participated and learned in worship rather than just 'sit and get' as is common in many worship services.

Educational theorists have long pointed out that we forget most of what we hear unless we also interact with the material visually, verbally or physically.[26] People who worship with a study guide in hand will experience increased recall and feel as if the Holy Spirit was speaking to them in worship.

Another benefit missional sermon-based small groups bring to worship is that they provide an opportunity for a church-wide focus on a particular issue or theme that pastors feel led to engage the congregation.

Early in the life of our new church, I felt led to craft a sermon series from the book of Jonah. I believed that the Lord wanted the DNA of our new church to be missional in nature.

I felt the story of Jonah would be a perfect book for everyone in the congregation to explore and discuss because Jonah is a story that reveals God's great love for the world while also exploring God's missional calling and our human confusion and reluctance to answer God's call.

After a five-week imersion of Jonah by our small but growing congregation, I could clearly see how hearts and minds were being transformed by the Holy Spirit. People were beginning to get what it meant to be "a blessing, the tangible touch of God to our neighbors." The only way such transformation happens is if the entire congregation is aligned and focused on one theme in its study, worship and fellowship. Stated simply, for five straight weeks, during a formative time in the life

26   Diane Cole, "A Message From Your Brain: I'm Not Good at Remembering What I Hear," *National Geographic*, March 13, 2014, https://www.nationalgeographic.com/science/article/140312-auditory-memory-visual-learning-brain-research-science .

of the congregation, we were all on the same page.

Still another benefit missional sermon-based small groups bring to worship is that they unite those who worship in-person with those who worship virtually and those who are traveling and away. Even before the pandemic, I heard many people say to me: "Doug, we will be away next Sunday, but we will be using our study guides and worshiping on-line." It's no secret that the pandemic has, in some cases, created two congregations; a virtual and an in-person congregation. Like me, you are probably wondering how to Bridge that gap and keep two congregations together?

Missional sermon-based small groups are one way to keep the congregation united and together in worship. Even if folks are uncomfortable worshiping in an in-person setting, they are probably more likely to join in a small group where the environment is smaller and safer.

Let me share two short anecdotes with you that highlight the benefits of missional sermon-based small groups in worship. Frequently, I hear from those who are active in small groups that they were so engaged in the sermon that they talked about the sermon and Scripture at lunch or later in the week with their spouse and family. Sometimes folks tell me that they have never felt comfortable talking theology or spirituality with anyone. But now that they are part of a small group, they have learned how to talk about things that are deeply personal and often vulnerable.

While, I have no hard numbers to back this up, I've had people tell me time and time again that they shortened their weekend plans in order to be back in time for Sunday worship because they didn't want to be away while their small group was meeting.

Let me be clear. The above stories don't happen every week. One reason is that I'm like most pastors. I'm neither a great preacher nor am I an especially dynamic presence in the pulpit. Yet, those stories illustrate the potential benefit that missional sermon-based small groups can offer a congregation.

THE BENEFITS MISSIONAL SERMON-BASED SMALL GROUPS HAVE FOR GROWING DISCIPLES

Missional sermon-based small groups foster a way of life together that grows disciples and nurtures the faith of a congregation. Those who participate in the small groups have an increasing exposure to God's Word. This, in turn, creates additional space for the Holy Spirit to work the lives of those in small groups.

Those active in the small groups often come to worship and small group more prepared because they know that the discussions are richer, deeper, and more authentic when participants are prepared. When each person is bringing their unique, Spirit-led insights to the study, lives are changed by the grace of God.

Finally, as I mentioned above, many people in our congregations are not comfortable sharing intimate and vulnerable details about faith and life with others. As facilitators create safe and open places for candid conversations, participants learn the language of faith and how to express that language out loud.

THE BENEFITS MISSIONAL SERMON-BASED SMALL GROUPS HAVE FOR MISSIONAL ENGAGEMENT

Missional sermon-based small groups foster a way of life together that increases the likelihood of members joining Jesus on mission in the neighborhoods around your church. I freely admit that my model for sermon-based small groups is not the only model, nor is it the best model. In fact, my model borrows heavily from Larry Osborne and his brilliant book Sticky Church.[27]

One of the unique aspects of my vision for small groups is how mission is incorporated into the larger rhythm of small group participation. Each missional sermon-based small group is encouraged to select their own mission to participate in during the small group series. As you can see in the structure of missional sermon-based small groups below, the opportunity to be on mission in one's neighborhood is central.

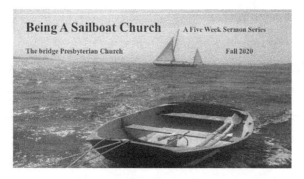

BEING A SAILBOAT CHURCH: I

CONNECTING WITH GOD'S PEOPLE

Getting to Know Each Other:

Welcome to our fall 2020 Sermon-Based Small Groups at the Bridge! Spend some time getting to know each other in your small group (if you don't already know each other). Share with the group your name and where you live.

Or share with the group an experience you've had either sailing or

27 Larry Osborne, *Sticky Church*, (Grand Rapids: Zondervan, 2008), 53.

rowing in a rowboat. Where were you? What was that like? Where were you going?

CONNECTING WITH GOD'S PASSION

Digging Deeper

1. What insight, principle, or observation from this weekend's message did you find to be most helpful, eye-opening, or troubling? Explain.

2. The earliest Christians chose a sailboat as a symbol for the church, because the earliest followers of Jesus understood that the Church was a God-powered, God-led and God-equipped adventure and the only way to be in relationship with Jesus, together, was by hoisting a sail and allowing themselves to be taken wherever the Lord wanted to take them.

- How do you react to the idea of our life together at the Bridge as an adventure with God?

- Discuss the differences that author Joan Gray points out below between a Sailboat Church and a Rowboat Church

The Rowboat Church

- Attitude = Either "WE can or WE can't do what God has called US to do."

- Progress = "Depends on circumstances like how much money do WE have or where is OUR location."

- Focus = "What can WE do with what WE have?"

The Sailboat Church

- Attitude = "GOD can do infinitely more than we can ask or imagine."

- Progress = "Because God leads and empowers us, what we lack in resources is not decisive to what God can accomplish in us.
- Focus = "What is God leading us to be and do now in the place where we find ourselves?"

3. <u>READ John 15: 1-11</u>: In John 15, Jesus uses an organic metaphor of being engrafted by the Father into the central vine, which is Jesus Christ.

- Share with the group any observations or questions you have. How does this metaphor help you understand what it means to 'abide in Jesus?'
- Central to the notion of 'abiding in Jesus' is the idea of being dependent upon our Lord, like a branch to a vine. How can the Bridge faithfully live in the tension between depending on Jesus yet not sitting idly by and doing nothing?

4. As Sailboat Churches abide with Jesus, the true vine, they learn how to let the Lord shape their desires; their decisions and their actions.

- Give examples of how has the Lord shaped your desires and decisions throughout your life?
- Give examples of how and where you see the Lord shaping the desires and decisions of the Bridge Presbyterian Church?

5. John 15: 5, NRSV: *"I am the vine, you are the branches. Those who abide in me and I in them bear much fruit, because apart from me you can do nothing."* What does Jesus mean when he said: *"Apart from me you can do nothing?"* What difference would it make in your life if you took very seriously these words of Jesus?

6. John 15:6: *"Whoever does not abide in me is thrown away like a branch and withers; such branches are gathered, thrown into the fire, and burned."* People in Sailboat Churches abide in Jesus and bear fruit or they get pruned and discarded. Where do you see the Bridge bearing fruit? How might the Lord be pruning the Bridge?

7. In marinas all around the world there are boats that seldom leave the dock. They remain tied up there, perhaps used as places to entertain or relax, even to live on, but their sails are rarely raised.

- How is the Bridge like a boat tied up in a marina and how is the Bridge like sailboat that has caught the wind of the Holy Spirit?
- How do you see the Bridge partnering with God? How do you experience yourself as a partner with God in God's work in the world?

Personal Application:

1. Doug ended the sermon with a call to recover the sailing life, challenging everyone to take three simple steps toward abiding with Jesus. Take time to consider (or discuss) each of the three steps:

- First, abide in Jesus by joining a small group.
- Second, pray. Pray for the Bridge; it's leaders; and for the leading of the Holy Spirit.
- Third, let go of your agendas and dreams for the Bridge and with renewed trust and dependence on the Holy Spirit, hoist the sails and follow where the wind leads.

2. Prayerfully consider how you can become more of a sailor and less of a rower in your spiritual life. Prayerfully consider how the Bridge can, together, become more of a Sailboat Church and less of a Rowboat Church.

CONNECTING WITH GOD'S PURPOSE

Our September featured Mission Partners: Matthew's Ministry and Charter Day School of Roger Bacon Academy. Matthew's Ministry provides food for local children so they have nourishment on weekends. Back-packs are needed to send the groceries home with them. The Bridge sponsors Town Creek Elementary and Charter Day School.

Charter Day School is in need of loose-leaf paper, one subject notebooks, glue sticks, pencil pouches, and erasers. If you feel called to support these ministries, a bin will be provided for your donations Monday, September 28, from 10:00-11:00 a.m.in front of the Bridge.

Monetary donations may be sent to the Bridge Presbyterian Church, 497 Olde Waterford Way,

Suite 205, Leland, NC, 28451, with "Matthew's Ministry" or "Charter Day School" on the memo line.

§

Specifically, each small group is encouraged to collaborate and pray about where and how the Lord might be leading the group to be on mission in the neighborhood. The goal is that by the end of the sermon series, each small group has either been on mission with the Lord by partnering with a particular mission agency or is planning on being on mission, together.

Early in the life of our congregation, one of our small groups had a brilliant idea. One of the members felt led to share with the group their involvement in a local mission organization called Brunswick Co Street Reach. Street Reach is an organization dedicated to caring for the homeless in Brunswick Co and run by an extraordinarily inspiring couple named Donna and Gary Phelps.

As this particular small group got more involved with Street Reach, it became clear to some of the small group members that the homeless in Brunswick Co often do not have a bed or mat to sleep on. This insight led to a brilliant idea by members of this small group. Why not collect the small plastic grocery bags and crochet them into sleep mats for the homeless?

Since that idea was birthed, the Bridge has made over 100 sleep mats which have been delivered to Street Reach, who in turn, gave the mats to some of their homeless clients.

Perhaps the greatest benefit associated with doing mission in small groups is illustrated by comparing how mission is traditionally been engaged in through the time honored all church mission project verses how mission is engaged in missional sermon-based small groups.

Let's imagine that it's Sunday morning at First Church. The elder or deacon who oversees the mission work of First church announces from the pulpit that on Saturday Sept 21st, the church will be coordinating their quarterly Habitat for Humanity work day. The leader goes on to remind the congregation that this is the tenth year First Church has partnered with Habitat for Humanity and together, First Church has helped build 6 homes in the downtown habitat village. "Please sign up in the foyer after worship," the leader says as he steps away from the pulpit.

Certainly, there is a lot to commend about this approach. First Church has faithfully built a number of affordable homes for worthy, yet under-resourced families. No doubt, some participants discovered how their skill sets helped care for the homeless and other participants unquestionably felt the great joy of participating in God's call to help the homeless. Perhaps, the faithful work with Habitat has helped First Church better understand it's God-given vocation.

However, if we take a moment to deconstruct the traditional way congregations engage in mission through all church mission projects, we will see some of the flaws of this increasingly outdated model. First, notice that all-church mission projects are typically chosen and organized by a few who are in leadership. Typically, members of the churches mission committee are the only ones who determine when mission is done, why it is done and where the church will be on mission with Jesus.

Second, the traditional all-church mission project is impersonal. Not only are few voices deciding when, where and how to be on mission with Jesus, but the particular mission project may or may not be a synergistic fit with the church members. Using the example above, I would not be very interested in participating in a Habitat for Humanity work day because, well, I'm not very handy (just ask my wife). However, I would be torn between doing what I thought was the right thing to do (be on mission with Jesus and my congregation) or skipping the work day because its not well suited for my particular gifts and passions.

In missional sermon-based small groups, time is dedicated in each small group session for the group to decide when, where and how the Lord is calling the group to be on mission. This means that everyone in the small group has input in selecting the mission project. Everyone is part of the decision. Thus, participant's identity more with the project because they have prayed and have a voice choosing which mission to partner with. Moreover, because everyone in the small group is part of the discussion of when, where and how to be on mission, there is a far greater chance everyone in the group will enthusiastically participate.

Additionally, participants are eager to share their story of being on mission with the rest of the congregation. Our practice at the Bridge is to have each small group tell their story about being on mission in Sunday worship. This is often done through words, pictures and video clips. As someone once told me after choosing and participating in mission with their small group: "This project is not just what we did. It's who we are becoming." That person was learning that they are part of the Body of Christ bearing witness to God's Kingdom in the neighborhood.

Finally, these small group mission projects increase the frequency in which folks in the congregation are on mission. They also tend to develop deeper relationships between small group members and they strengthen the partnership between the congregation the mission agency the small group has chosen to work with.

One word of caution, however. We've learned that some small groups agonize over the decision of when and how to be on mission, together. They find it very difficult to identify their group mission project. So, our small group team decided to give the small groups the option of prayerfully choosing which sustainable partnership to be on mission with OR having the mission team suggest a sustainable partnership. Therefore, at the beginning of each sermon-based small group series there is a suggested sustainable partnership that is provided to each group in the study guide.

THE BENEFITS MISSIONAL SERMON-BASED SMALL GROUPS HAVE FOR PROMOTING ORGANIC, BOTTOM-UP MOVEMENTS OF THE HOLY SPIRIT

One of the most surprising, yet exciting discoveries we've had with our missional sermon-based small groups is how we've sensed the Holy Spirit moving in organic ways. Perhaps the best way to describe this phenomenon is through stories of how Jesus is at work calling people into mission through small groups at the Bridge.

Bettye and her husband Ed joined our congregation early on. One day, while attending a small group, Bettye overheard a conversation about our mission involvement with Kids World Academy – a school for pre-kindergarten students whose families are living below the poverty line. During that conversation, Bettye felt the Holy Spirit calling her to take a leadership role in nurturing the relationship between our church and Kids World Academy.

Greer and her husband Tom have been active in local missions throughout their adult lives. Shortly after joining the Bridge Presbyterian Church, Greer joined a small group and through that small group became interested in volunteering at a food pantry sponsored by Brunswick Family Assistance. Every Thursday morning Greer and Tom gather food at the local grocery stores and then deliver the food to the food bank.

Over time, Greer became the elder for small groups at the Bridge and Tom has been a facilitator. These are examples of how the Spirit moves within small groups to raise up women and men to join Jesus on mission in our city.

THE BENEFITS MISSIONAL SERMON-BASED SMALL GROUPS HAVE FOR IDENTIFYING FACILITATORS.

If you've ever tried to organize a small group ministry you've likely realized that one of the greatest challenges is finding, training and keeping small group leaders. Some refer to the challenge as the bane of their small group ministry.

Missional sermon-based small groups make finding and keeping leaders much easier. The most obvious reason for this is because all the leader needs to do is show up on Sunday and the day of the small group. There is no formal preparation time needed to be a missional sermon-based small group facilitator. There is no need for the facilitator to crack open a Bible commentary or concordance. Additionally, there is no formal or semi-formal biblical or theological training needed to facilitate. This makes attracting and keeping facilitators much easier.

That said, many leaders re-read a hard copy of the sermon that I provide prior to the small group study. Some are motivated to study and learn more but that motivation is organic, and Spirit-led. Because the study guide that I provide in advance always has more questions than time will allow to answer, the biggest challenge for most leaders is to pick and choose which questions they want to research more, if they want to do that.

FOUR CHARACTERISTICS OF MISSIONAL SERMON-BASED SMALL GROUPS THAT MAKE ALL THE DIFFERENCE

Missional Sermon-based small groups can be exciting, transformational and Spirit-infused. But they should never be confused with the ultimate goal of any congregation. Instead, missional sermon-based small groups should be understood as a tool the Lord of the Church can use to draw people into deeper union with Jesus and to help foster a deeper, more Kingdom-oriented life together. I believe there are four characteristics not exclusively, but uniquely found in small groups that help foster a deeper, more Kingdom-oriented life together.

Characteristic #1: Honesty/Authenticity - Essential for fostering a deeper more Kingdom-oriented life together is honesty and transparency. Just stand around the foyer or the parking lot of any church on a given Sunday and listen to how God's people greet one another. You'll hear numerous varieties of "What up? How you doing?" But no matter how good or bad things may be for a particular parishioner, more than likely, she or he will respond by saying: "I'm fine."

It doesn't matter if one's marriage is falling apart; if the kids broke curfew for the third night in a row or if someone is about to lose their job. The answer is the same. "I'm Fine." Lots of times "How you doing?" just means "I see you." We don't really want or expect an answer. No wonder the stereotype of many churches is that they are a place with lots of inauthentic smiles.[28]

Missional sermon-based small groups change that because they are structured to naturally foster greater honesty and transparency. We learned that it's better for small groups to meet in people's homes. With the threat of the pandemic lingering, meeting in small groups may be even more attractive to participants. Additionally, we try keep the small groups to 10 -12 people. Remaining small and meeting in the comfort of people's homes make things more conducive to authenticity.

Larry Osborne puts it this way: Would you be more likely to be open and honest?

1. In a living room or a classroom?

2. In a group where there's always a new face, or a group where

28   Larry Osborne, *Sticky Church*, (Grand Rapids: Zondervan, 2008), 53.

you already know everyone?

3.   With twelve or with 25 people?[29]

Characteristic #2: Belonging - Essential for fostering a deeper more Kingdom-oriented life together is a sense of belonging. Creating space for people to belong is the postmodern onramp to a life of faith. One recent study showed that for more than 60% of people, the Sunday morning worship gathering is no longer the primary on-ramp to a life of faith.[30] Simply put: People don't see church attendance making any difference in the lives of most Christians they know, so they aren't inclined to go to church.

That said, what non-Christian seekers are looking for is a sense of belonging. This is especially true for younger believers and seekers. They don't much care about what we believe (that's hard for us Presbyterians to accept) until they know how much we care. What seekers are looking for when they give our churches a try is a sense of belonging.

My friend Mark Tidsworth tells of a large church that needed a new drummer for its praise band. They were focused on quality, so they hired a gifted musician. This young adult was not a Christ-follower, but was open to playing for worship services after he completed his sets at clubs on Saturday nights.

Predictably, after about a year, he became tired of playing late into Saturday nights and then early Sunday mornings. He talked with his wife about the need to quit one of these gigs. To his surprise, she quickly said, "Quit the clubs." He was confused at her suggestion, since she had no personal investment in the church job.

Why?" he asked. "Because I like you so much better since you started playing in that praise band." After brief reflection this young

---

29   Osborne, *Sticky Church*, 54.
30   Kelly Hartnett, Your Church is More Than a Worship Service: Finding Other On-Ramps, *Church Marketing Sucks.* September 10, 2014, http://churchmarketingsucks. com/2014/09/your-church-is-more-than-a-worship-service-finding-other-on-ramps/

man responded, "You know, I think I'm one of them now. I think I've become one of those Christian people."[31]

Characteristic #3: Accountability - Accountability is essential in order to foster a deeper, more Kingdom-oriented life together. Most Christians want to do more reading of the bible, praying, reaching out to meet needs in the community, right? Similarly, most churches want to be filled with those type people. But busy schedules and lack of commitment conspire to keep this from happening. This is why accountability is so important.

Small groups ensure that a wide swath of the church is praying, studying Scripture and caring for each other throughout the week. The invisible thread weaving all this together is an unspoken sense of accountability.

Characteristic #4: Empowerment - Key to fostering a deeper, more Kingdom-oriented life together is empowerment. Small groups unleash mission and ministry in people's lives. In his book Sticky Church, Larry Osborne suggests that there are two myths Small Group ministry undercuts. The first myth is: The Holy Person Myth – the idea of pastors and clergy having a more direct line to God.[32]

As missional sermon-based small groups pop up within your congregation, you'll realize that small groups meet in a wide variety of settings making it impossible for the pastor to be everywhere to carry out all pastoral roles. This means two things: 1) People within the small groups begin taking on the responsibility of caring for each other; praying for each other; wrestling with theological questions together; and taking God's Kingdom to the neighborhood. This frees the pastor up to do the things she or he is uniquely qualified to do

At the Bridge, we realized that lay people often offer much better

31   Mark Tidsworth, SHIFT, 57.
32   Osborne, Sticky Church, 47-52.

care for each other than I ever could as their pastor. One small group organized meals for a month to one member who underwent a difficult surgical procedure. Another small group helped a retired clergy couple get over the deep wounds of being betrayed by a former congregation. Missional sermon-based small groups have the potential to unleash ministry among lay people and renew faith of new and long-time congregants and…the pastor doesn't have to do that work.

The second myth Osborne suggests that small group ministry undercuts is: The Holy Place Myth. This is the myth that God's presence is greater or more accessible is some places than others. Because small groups typically meet outside the wall of the church building, people begin seeing God at work in their homes, living rooms, they start to realize that God is just as likely to show up anywhere.[33]

Friends, let's face it, in most churches there aren't that many opportunities for high impact, life on life ministry. Sure, some people teach or lead worship or volunteer for youth ministry. But most roles are of the supporting-cast-variety, designed to keep the machine running instead of making a difference the lives of the congregation and the neighborhood. Small groups empower people for the type of ministry that makes a difference.

TESTING OUR SUNDAY SCHOOL MODELS

When I have led workshops on missional sermon-based small groups, the conversations before and after the workshop lead to participants re-thinking and re-visioning Sunday school and other small groups in the church. Perhaps reading this book has forced you to re-think the Sunday school model that is operating within your congregation.

Even if you feel the traditional model of Sunday school is tired, outdated and needing to be blown up, chances are there are folks in

---

33   Ibid.

your congregation who do not share your vision. If you are considering re-tooling or re-examining your Sunday School program or if you want to prepare your leadership team for a conversation about the utility of Sunday school, then here are a few things to consider.

A functional starting point for exploring the usefulness of the traditional adult Sunday school model is found in this question: Does our current model of adult Sunday school fit our God-given purpose? Many adult Sunday schools are long-standing, pillars of the church. They have blessed and nurtured the saints for years. Not only has the adult Sunday school program been around longer than most can remember, but many participants in the adult Sunday school classes have been participating for 10 – 15 or even 20 years.

This means that primary friendships have been formed in these classes. Powerful experiences of the Holy Spirit have been shared. Some classes are even named in memory of a beloved leader. All that being said, every adult Sunday school class, like every other ministry, mission and activity in a local church must stand up to the scrutiny of this question; Does this fit our God-given purpose?

Questions You Can Use to Review Your Adult Sunday School Model

Here are some important questions to ask as you review your current adult Sunday school program. I call these Sunday School Pinch Points:

- IS Sunday School designed mostly for members or does the program connect with non-members?
- IS Sunday School designed for Sunday morning or does the church offer Christian formation on days not called Sunday?
- DOES Sunday School lead to hands on, missional engagement

that makes a difference or does Sunday School lack opportunities to make a difference in the neighborhood?

- IF we did not do Sunday School already, would we, knowing what we now know, launch Sunday School

- IS Sunday School helping us achieve our ultimate purpose?

- How is Sunday School making disciples?

- Would your decision to let go or continue Sunday School be based primarily on the perceived level of conflict the decision will create?

- How will Sunday School bless God's mission at St. Andrews in five and ten years.

- Does Sunday School sustain the organization or does it grow God's mission?

In his book: <u>A Year with Jesus: Daily Readings and Meditations,</u> author Eugene Peterson begins one of his devotions by citing Matthew 11: 28-30, NRSV: 'Come to me, all you that are weary and are carrying heavy burdens, and I will give you rest. Take my yoke upon you, and learn from me; for I am gentle and humble in heart, and you will find rest for your souls. For my yoke is easy, and my burden is light.'

Then, commenting on this passage, Peterson writes: Jesus doesn't ask us to do anything that he doesn't promise to do with us. *We are not so much sent out as invited along.*"[34] Do you sense the Holy Spirit doing a new thing in your congregation? Has the pandemic created space for innovation and change? Is the Lord of the Church "inviting you along" as Christ prepares the congregation to make the shift to missional sermon-based small groups?

---

34 Eugene Peterson, *A Year with Jesus: Daily Readings and Meditations*, (New York: Harper Collins, 2006), p 117.

CHAPTER THREE

THE USE OF QUESTIONS IN PREACHING: HOW TO DEVELOP INTERACTIVE SERMONS THAT KEEP PEOPLE'S ATTENTION

In Chapter three, I will discuss the use of questions in preaching. This chapter is written primarily for pastors, lay preachers as well as elders and deacons who lead worship teams. However, it also provides insights and creative material for anyone interested in faithful ways to grow congregational engagement during Sunday worship.

The Use of Questions In Preaching:

How to Develop Interactive Sermons That Keep People's Attention

To those who regularly prepare sermons and fill pulpits in Sunday worship, see if you can relate to this. It's early Sunday morning. You're particularly excited about preaching the sermon – increasingly convinced that the message will be enthusiastically received. Then, you get into the pulpit and about half way through the sermon you feel it. Despite your best homiletical efforts and despite what you think is some of the most creative and inspiring sermon content, you've lost em! The congregation is just not with you.

Learning to how to use questions while you preach is a simple but effective way to keep the congregation's attention throughout the sermon. Learning the art of asking the right question; the right way at the right time is a homiletical tool that will help to keep the congregation engaged.

Have you ever felt like the traditional twenty to thirty-minute sermon; a form of communication that was minted when radio was king, is out of touch within the interactive world that we live in? Let's face it, it is! In a society where news channels invite us to interactive town halls and social medium platforms encourage feedback, chat rooms and ongoing interaction, the idea of standing in front of a group of people and expecting them to sit still; stay quiet; and simply listen – to the same voice, at the same time, every week is an impossible task.

Discussion Questions:

1. How does it feel knowing that it is not only likely, it's inevitable that your congregation will tune out some, most or all of that sermon you worked on for 12 – 18 hours

2. What sort of expectations does your congregation have for the preaching of God's Word on Sunday morning?

No matter how talented an orator you may be, listeners in your congregation will lose focus. Regardless of how compelling the content of your sermon is, listeners in Sunday worship will mentally wander off. And for good reason.

Consider this statistic: A recent Microsoft consumer study claims the human attention span today is 8 seconds, down from 12 seconds in 2000. The goldfish has an attention span of 9 seconds.[35] So, unless we are preaching in an aquarium to a room full of goldfish, we need to find ways to keep our congregation engaged.

How does it feel knowing that it is not just likely, but it's inevitable that your congregation will tune out some, most or all of that sermon you worked on for 12–18 hours?

I would like to offer suggestions for how to intentionally engage the congregation during the worship service. How do you feel about the notion of encouraging interaction during the proclamation of the Word? Does that sound scary...maybe you're thinking that things could quickly get out of control?

Perhaps, the idea intrigues you, but you're pretty sure your congregation would have a hard time adjusting to a more interactive format? Perhaps you are energized about the idea of interacting with the congregation thinking: *"Yea, that's what is missing in Sunday worship."* Here's an idea to consider. Try introducing questions into the rhythm of your worship service.

WHY SHOULD YOU ASK QUESTIONS IN WORSHIP?

Asking the congregation intentional, well-planned questions, instantly hooks them into the sermon. Over time, asking the congregation questions on a regular basis creates a sense of anticipation in the listeners. Asking the congregation questions in worship creates unique, but comfortable space for the Holy Spirit to engage the congregation.

35   Kevin McSpadden, "You Now Have a Shorter Attention Span Than a Goldfish," *Time*, May 14, 2015, https://time.com/3858309/attention-spans-goldfish/

Within the Reformed, Presbyterian tradition that I am part of, we believe that the Holy Spirit is at work in that space between the preaching and the hearing of God's Word. Therefore, questions are a faithful way for preachers to invite listeners to inhabit that space where the Spirit is at work.

Congregational questions prepare those in worship for the interaction between biblical text and real life. Remember when sermons were critiqued by the amount of their theological content? Well today, all the creative and well-articulated theological content in the world will not suffice without the sermon answering the question: How do I apply this to my life? Well-placed, theologically grounded questions help listeners in worship to answer that question. More importantly, asking good questions allows the congregation to Bridge Scripture to their daily living rather than putting that burden on the preacher.

Why Should You Ask Questions In Worship?

Asking the congregation intentional, well-planned questions, instantly hooks them into the sermon.

Over time, asking the congregation questions creates a sense of anticipation in the listeners.

Asking the congregation questions in worship creates unique, but comfortable space for the Holy Spirit to engage the congregation.

Congregational Questions prepare those in worship for the interaction between biblical text and real life.

Discussion Questions:

1. What kind of interaction do you have with your congregation on a typical Sunday? Is it spontaneous or intentional?

2. Have you ever asked the congregation a question from the pulpit? What happened?

3. How does the congregation respond to opportunities to interact with you during worship and especially during the sermon?

WHAT ARE THE RIGHT TYPE OF QUESTIONS TO ASK?

Developing questions to be asked in worship begins while crafting the sermon. As I'm writing the sermon, I look for moments within the manuscript that lend themselves to questions. If you try developing this discipline, you'll be surprised how many times in the writing of your sermon, you will uncover potential questions you might want to stop and ask your congregation.

I typically focus on three to four questions per sermon. The first question acts to hook the congregation into the sermon. Questions I have asked recently at the beginning of the sermon include: "When was the last time you went to a costume party?" "What emotions is the pandemic flattening in your life right now?"

The second question invites the congregation to dive deeper into the text. Questions I've asked lately include: "Why do you think the Lord told Jeramiah to go

What Are the Right Type of Questions To Ask?

The first question acts like a hook:

"When was the last time you went to a costume party?"

The second question invites the congregation to dive deeper into the text:

"Why do you think the Lord told Jeremiah to go down to the potter's house?"

The final question needs to be about personal application:

"How can you rise above your pain and share the love of Christ with others this week?"

down to the potter's house?" Or "Is faith more like a race we must win or is faith more about simply finishing...never giving up?

The final question needs to be about personal application. Examples of that type of question include: "How can you rise above your pain and share the love of Christ with others this week?"

As far as developing the specific questions, sometimes the questions naturally emerge as I am writing the sermon while other times I read over the sermon and determine questions that I want to ask the congregation. The main thing to anticipate as you develop the discipline of asking congregational questions is that you will find a fascinating dialogue emerging during your sermon preparation.

The internal dialogue going on during the crafting of the sermon is between You – the preacher; The Word of God and The Congregation. When I write the sermon, I find myself wondering: What might the congregation need greater clarity on or what do I want the congregation to pay special attention to – then I turn those into questions.

If you try this and have trouble imagining when and how to insert a question into the body of a sermon, then imagine you are reading the sermon to your spouse or a friend or a leader in your congregation. As you are reading the sermon, notice those moments when you might want to go 'off script' and ask the imaginary listener a thought provoking or provocative question.

Another way to cultivate the habit developing questions while writing your sermon is to think about your congregation while writing. You know them well enough to anticipate the sort of questions they might be asking themselves as they listen to the sermon. They may be confused about a particularly loaded theological word or concept. That would be an appropriate time to work a question into the body of the sermon.

I am convinced that is part of the preaching task for us who are living in an interactive world with an increasingly short attention span. Asking the congregation questions is an intentional (albeit a rhetorical) devise designed to put the congregation in direct interaction with the Word of God.

A QUESTION RECENTLY ASKED DURING WORSHIP: AN EXAMPLE

I recently asked the congregation at the church I'm privileged to serve this question: *"As Peter walked on the water, what was it that made Peter afraid causing him to sink?"* The assumption is that it was the water crashing around Peter's legs that created his fear. But, curiously, Matthew records in 14:30: "But when Peter noticed the strong wind, he became frightened, and he began to sink."

In asking the question, I wanted to make the point that we are at our best as a church and people of faith when the wind of the Holy Spirit is at our back. So, when the wind is against us, we need to cry out just like Peter: "Lord, save me." The question I asked put the congregation in dialogue with the Word of God helping them to better see the point I was making.

Discussion Questions:

1. Think back to the last few sermons you preached. If possible, think about a question you would have liked to ask the congregation?

2. What potential benefits might you find from asking that question?

WHEN AND HOW SHOULD YOU ENGAGE THE CONGREGATION WITH QUESTIONS?

Here's what I do. After our opening prayers, music, confession and passing of the peace, I enter the pulpit and begin by asking my three questions. Typically, I project them on the screens and they scroll one at a time. But if you don't have screens, you can print your questions in the Sunday bulletin. After asking the questions, I pray, I read scripture and I begin the sermon.

I always ask the questions prior to praying for God to bless the reading and hearing of God's Word because the questions, automatically, perk congregational interest. Putting your questions to the congregation prior to reading Scripture allows the questions to do their job – which is to be used by the Holy Spirit to draw the congregation into the conversation between them and the Word. Additionally, asking the congregation questions will develop rapport with the listeners.

The key to keeping the congregation engaged is to refer back to the questions during the sermon. I make sure I ask the questions before Scripture is read and then repeat the questions within the body of the sermon. For example, I might say: *"Earlier I asked you the question: How in the world could Mary and Joseph lose track of their son on the way back to Nazareth?"* I have learned that referring back to the questions I asked earlier in worship, keeps the congregation engaged and functions as a segue into your next point while also helping to illuminate a biblical truth.

The Emerging Dialogue When Asking Congregational Questions?

You – the preacher

The Word of God ------- The Congregation

Occasionally, I ask the final question (which typically focuses on personal application) during the benediction or final blessing. It may sound something like this: *"As you go into the world, ask yourself: How can*

I be a blessing, the tangible touch of God to others."

When and How Should You Engage The Congregation With Questions?

Questions

Prayer

Scripture Reading

Sermon

Final Blessing
(refer back to question)

SHOULD INTERACTION BE ENCOURAGED?

You can play this by ear. As you begin introducing questions in worship, you'll likely find that people will treat them as rhetorical questions – that is good questions designed to make a point rather than be answered out loud. If you want to develop the technique of asking questions to the congregation during worship but don't know how to being, try something like: *"OK, I'm going to try something new in worship for the next few months. I'm going to be asking you questions before the sermon. These questions aren't designed to be answered out loud but to help you engage in God's Word."*

If you can foster the habit of asking questions in worship, you will find that over time, folks just can't resist answering some questions out loud. I encourage you not to silence that congregational impulse. Hearing occasion responses from the congregation can be fun. More importantly, it can be instructive for you and empowering to the congregation.

Growing up in Wisconsin made me a huge Green Bay Packers football fan. Occasionally, I will read a chat about the Packers in the local Milwaukee newspaper. They are typically hosted by one of the sports writers on the staff of the paper. I'll never forget that at the end of a long chat transcript, a relatively new sports reporter told the chat audience how reluctant he was to engage in online chats. However, he discovered that during the chats, he has learned what questions his readers are wrestling with about the Packers. The questions his audience is asking often inform what he chooses to write about in his weekly column.

See the spontaneous questions the congregation might ask in worship as a window into where they are at, spiritually and theologically. If, as you develop the practice of asking questions in worship, the congregational responses get to crazy or silly, just remember that you can control the amount of interaction. The congregation will be in training with you – learning how to ask and respond to questions, together. The responses will range from an occasional spontaneous response to you actively soliciting answers.

Should Interaction Be Encouraged?

"OK, I'm going to try something new in worship for the next few months. I'm going to be asking you questions before the sermon. These questions aren't designed to be answered out loud but to help you engage in God's Word."

Discussion Questions:

1. What are some steps you might take to begin developing the practice of asking the congregation questions before and during the sermon?

2. Is there a committee or team you would need to educate or get approval from prior to you beginning to ask question in

worship?

3. Is there a small group of folks who could come along side you and help you develop questions?

I've turned the art of asking questions in worship into what has become the backbone of the Bridge Presbyterian Church – missional sermon-based Small Groups. Typically, the three questions I ask before and during the sermon are part of our missional sermon-based small group studies that meet weekly in people's homes.

CHAPTER FOUR

MISSIONAL SERMON-BASED SMALL GROUP SERMONS AND STUDY GUIDES

By now you are probably ready to take the next step to begin developing missional-sermon based small groups in your congregation. But you're saying to yourself: "One thing that would really help is if I could sit in on a small group and observe all that goes on." I get that. I wish I could provide you with a digital way of looking in on one of our small groups. But one of the basic tenants of our small groups is confidentiality.

Not only that, but each small group is different and it would be unwise and unfair to provide you with a link to a YouTube video of a small group precisely because each group is unique. So, it wouldn't be wise to make one example of small group life normative because every group is different and…every group is messy!

I am currently finishing developing a sermon series on the seven churches that John addressed in the book of Revelation. Eugene Peterson offers this astute observation about the seven churches. "The churches of the Revelation show us that churches are not Victorian parlors where everything is always picked up and ready for guests. They are messy family rooms…things are out of order, to be sure, but that's what happens to churches that are lived in."[36]

Peterson is spot on. The church I serve, like the church you are a part of, is full of imperfect people with their own unique way of being

---

36   Eugene Peterson, *Reversed Thunder* (New York: Harper Collins, 1998), 54.

a lampstand for Christ. I think it would be a disservice for anyone to look in on another small group and decide: "OK, that's the way things SHOULD be done." Each church is different. Each possesses its own strengths and weaknesses. Each church is a unique product of its environment, history, theology and vision.

So, instead of offering you a sneak peek into one of our missional sermon-based small groups, I encourage you to anticipate and celebrate how the Spirit is working within your unique, one-of-a-kind congregation.

Also, please keep in mind that there is not an ideal size or type of congregation that is more or less suitable for the formation of missional sermon-based small groups. All that is needed are people eager to follow the Holy Spirit and unafraid to try something new. That said, some who read this book are convinced that this type of small group could be a good fit for their congregation, nonetheless, the timing is just not right – perhaps because of an ongoing conflict or a slow post-pandemic bounce back.

Listen again to Eugene Peterson's observation about the seven churches addressed in Revelation. Peterson writes: "There is no evidence in the annals of ancient Israel or in the pages of the New Testament that churches were ever much better or much worse than they are today. A random selection of seven churches in any century, including our own, would turn up something very much like the seven churches to which St. John was pastor."[37]

Simply put, don't wait for the right time to develop missional sermon-based small groups or until your congregation is free from challenges and setbacks. Your church is not much better or much worse than any other. The question for you and your team is this: Is the Holy Spirit leading us to develop this type of small group ministry in our congregation?

37   Peterson, *Reversed Thunder*, 56.

So, while I can't provide you with an inside look into an actual small group, I can provide you with examples of sermons and corresponding study guides that I have developed and used. In the space below you will find examples of two sermons along with their corresponding study guides.

I feel a bit queasy offering examples of my sermons for the general public to read...and likely critique (so please be gentle). But I do so with the hope that you will see that an imperfect sermon written by an imperfect pastor accompanied by an imperfect study guide can still bear fruit in the lives of one's congregation.

The first example I am providing comes from the series I wrote years ago titled: Eight Words To Pray Every Day.

First, you will read a brief description of the series that I wrote for the congregation.

Second, you'll be able to peruse an example of a sermon from that series.

Third, you will be able to view the small group study guide that corresponds to the sermon. Notice how the study guide is divided into three sections in order to integrate time for fellowship; time for prayer; time for Bible study and time to plan for going on mission with Jesus. Notice also, how I craft questions for group discussion and personal application. Finally, notice how I intentionally plant questions in the body of the sermon that I use in the study guide.

EIGHT WORDS TO PRAY EVERY DAY:
DESCRIPTION OF THE SERIES

This is an example of how I create buzz and interest around the sermon series. I create a sermon series icon that we use in-house and on social media. Additionally, I try to craft a description of the series that will draw people into deeper interaction with God's Word while also seeing how the series has personal application.

EIGHT WORDS TO PRAY EVERY DAY

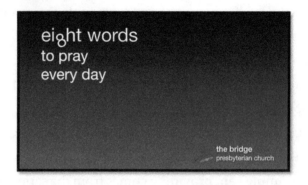

*"Better a single word spoken from a heart of love **than a thousand from a heart of indifference."*** Evagrius Ponticus.

Maybe your spiritual life is on autopilot and you're going through the motions. Perhaps you're keeping the religious treadmill spinning, but your soul is empty or tired. Or maybe your relationship with the Lord has fallen victim to the *'Too's'* - *too* many other obligations... *too* much guilt...*too* many changes in life; ...*too* many questions... *too* much pain...*too* much disappointment.

However, you're still asking: *"How can I experience a life with God day by day?"* What if there were eight simple words that, when prayed every day, help you genuinely connect with God? <u>Eight Words to Pray Every Day</u> is a new sermon series that transforms eight ordinary words into one-word prayers. Each of these words are simple, practical and, most of all, reliable.

If you struggle to start or keep connected with the Lord, or if your fast-pace lifestyle makes it hard to find daily time for the Lord, <u>Eight Words to Pray Every Day</u> can change your life; and draw you closer to the Lord. Beginning Labor Day weekend, each week a new word will be unveiled in worship and discussed in small groups. Join us as we learn to pray <u>Eight Words to Pray Every Day.</u>

EIGHT WORDS TO PRAY EVERY DAY: SERMON EXAMPLE

Here is an example of week I sermon in the sermon series: <u>Eight Words to Pray Every Day</u>. Within the sermon manuscript, I have kept the insertions where I call for a slide to put up on the screen. We utilize big screens in worship and I always provide a few power-point slides so that listeners are able to interact with the material auditorily and visually. You will also see where I have included specific questions in the body of the sermon that will find their way into the study guide.

<u>The First Word: HERE</u>
<u>Eight Words to Pray Every Day</u>
<u>A Sermon Preached from the Pulpit of</u>
<u>The Bridge Presbyterian Church</u>

"Zacchaeus, hurry and come down; for I must stay at your house today." Luke 19:5, NRSV

(Slide #2) The first church I served, First Presbyterian Church of Deerfield, IL, was a huge, neo-Gothic church in the northern suburbs of Chicago. I was called to be the youth minister and part of my compensation included living in a renovated one-bed apartment inside the church. And in case you're wondering the answer is 'yes,' living in a church will definitely put a dent in one's dating life. But, by and large, it was pretty cool living in the church.

The only problem with living in that church was that First Pres was a vibrant place filled with dynamic people. So, the church was seldom empty. But when the people finally cleared out and the long days of ministry were over, First Pres, became this dark and shadowy place, eerily silent and a bit imposing to walk through.

(Slide #3) Because the church was a vast three-story labyrinth of rooms, corridor and sacred spaces, I never knew who might be lurking in the building. So, not wanting to scare anyone, I started the habit of whistling whenever I walked through the dark hallways late at night.

Whistling was my way of communicating into the dark unknown: "I'm here." It was also my way of calling out into those creepy corridors: "Is anyone else here?" Sometimes, I'd forget to whistle while strolling through the dark, empty church and I'd occasionally, hear a panicky voice from out of the darkness ask: "Who's here?" I'd typically laugh out loud, announce myself and then we'd chat it up for a while.

The word "here" is a word that starts a conversation and a relationship. Whether calling out to someone or answering someone's call, the word "here" makes a connection; it breaks through isolation as if to say: "yep, I am present."

(Slide #4) The first word to pray every single day is the word "here." As for me, I'm trying to make the word "here" be the first word I say every morning of every new day. Really, it's kind of cool to think about the word "here" being the first audible sound that comes out of your mouth in the morning.

But because I'm saying that word out loud, I'm assuming I'm communicating to the Lord. So every morning I say "here," I'm also making an affirmation that our Lord is also "here," listening…even waiting to hear from me.

So, praying the word "here" every morning, we begin the day saying: "I am present in God's presence." (Question #1 is underlined)

<u>Imagine how your life might change for the better if</u> even - before that first hot sip of fresh-brewed coffee touches your lips or the warm water-pellets of the shower cascade across your back - the very first thing you utter out loud is a one-word prayer: "here!"

"Here" is not only a declaration it's also a response. (Slide #5) Remember growing up when that substitute teacher showed up in math class and the first thing she did was roll call? You remember that, right? Do you remember how you responded when your name was called? It was (what)… "Here!" When I pray the word 'here' every morning, it's also a response to God who, through Jesus Christ, started this whole relationship with me – and with all of us.

It's all pretty cool to consider who initiated the relationship between us humans and God. Think about this: We didn't create ourselves, right? God took the initiative to create us. We didn't decide to send Jesus into the world in the form of an infant, did we? God took that initiative to send Jesus to be God in real-time to us.

We didn't decide to have Jesus die for us and rise again, right? Our Lord took the initiative to die for the sin of the world. None of us sought out a relationship with the risen Lord. It was the Lord who sought us out, made himself so real to us that we were compelled to accept him as Lord and Savior, right?

So…to begin each day with the simple prayer, "here," is our response to the Great Initiator who created us, saved us, found us, daily seeks us out and never ever gives up on us. Throughout the Bible, it's God who takes the initiative to start a relationship with us humans – often calling us by name.

One example is found in the story of King David. During this series, I'm going to weave different stories from the life of King David into each sermon. (Slide #6) I'm grateful to the book <u>Leap Over A Wall</u> by Eugene Peterson for inspiration and insights. I've chosen the story of

David because, while he was a king, he's a lot like us. So, each week, I'm going to connect a different story from the life of David to one of the eight unique words to pray every day.

It's worth noting that the David narrative in I and II Samuel is a story of a layperson who lives a remarkable life of faith. David wasn't ordained to the priesthood. He wasn't called to the ministry. He was an ordinary person like everyone in this room not named Rev. Wes or Dr. Doug (or Rick Howell). The story opens with some important historical information. Israel's King, Saul, had disobeyed God. A new King was needed.

Samuel, the Prophet, was instructed by God to go to Bethlehem and invite a man named Jesse and his sons to make a sacrifice to God. Somehow in that process, God promised to show Samuel, God's choice to be the new King of Israel.

One by one Jesse paraded his sons in front of Samuel but as each son passed by, the Prophet Samuel heard the Lord say: "nope, that's not my anointed one." Finally, Samuel asked Jesse if he had anymore sons. Jesse said that his youngest was out watching the sheep in the field (never even mentioning the boy's name). Jesse fetched the unnamed boy and when he arrived on the scene the voice of the Lord instructed Samuel to "arise and anoint him, for this is the one," still never mentioning the boy's name.

Finally, in the last verse of this story we learn that the spirit of the Lord mightily came upon this boy and chose him. The unnoticed and uninvited shepherd boy, was now anointed and named; David! David's name is mentioned at the end of the story to emphasize that God seeks us out...by name. And the shepherd boy, David, shows us that the most basic response to God's call is to just show up; just be present; just say "here!"

It is but one of many stories where God calls to us by name. Look at Genesis 3: 8-9. Adam and Eve are fresh off the worst mistake they could have made. They disobeyed God by eating the forbidden fruit. Intuitively, they knew they had seriously damaged the relationship with God. So, they ran and they hid from God. But then...but then they heard the sound of the Lord God walking in the garden in the cool of the evening breeze, calling to them by name, saying: "Adam, Adam... where are you?"

Friends, when we run from God – even out of guilt or shame - it's God who takes the initiative to chase after us and call us by name. And all God wants to hear from us is a simple one-word response. Anyone wanna guess what that word is? The word is: "here."

Look at Isaiah 6:8. Isaiah has this stunning vision of the most-high God. Isaiah is overwhelmed by the glory of God and feels utterly, totally and completely unworthy. Yet, in verse 8 Isaiah records: "Then I heard the voice of the Lord saying, 'Whom shall I send, and who will go for us?'" And I said, "Here...here am I; send me!"

Even when we feel unworthy or undeserving, it's God who takes the initiative to chase after us, often calling us by name, all the while waiting to hear one word from us: "Here."

In our gospel story, Jesus is passing through the town of Jericho. Within that town was a man named Zacchaeus. He was a chief tax collector. Now tax collectors systematically extorted money from the Jewish people. So, they were despised in much the same way people today despise someone like Bernie Madoff.

But a chief tax collector was hated even more than the tax collectors because the chief tax collector oversaw the entire system of taxation in a given town – and became wealthy off the backs of the people being extorted.

Zacchaeus was, likely, the most despised, most rejected and loneliest man in Jericho – and for good reason. Yet, Zacchaeus somehow felt compelled to check out this itinerant holy man named Jesus as he passed through the dusty streets of Jericho. So, what did he do? (Question#2) <u>Why do you think Zacchaeus climbed that tree</u>? Scripture says it was because he was short and wanted to get a better look at Jesus. But I think there may have been another reason why he climbed the sycamore tree.

(Slide # 7) I saw this the other day on Facebook, "It Costs $0.00 to be a decent human being." I thought to myself what a useless post. My guess is that most people reading that post don't need to be inspired toward decency because they already think they are pretty decent human beings. But Zacchaeus was not like most of us. He knew he was immoral and that his shady treatment of others caused untold pain and suffering.

I'm told that the sycamore tree bears enormously large leaves; large enough that one could safely hide in sycamore tree nearly concealed from the foot traffic below. If that's the case, I imagine short, little Zacchaeus tucked away in a blooming sycamore tree desperately wanting Jesus to see him, yet too ashamed…too riddled with self-loathing to say anything.

Somehow Jesus saw Zacchaeus buried in the leaves, and called him… called him <u>by name</u>. "Zacchaeus," Jesus called out and I imagine the stunned tax collector involuntarily putting the palm of his hand over his chest and with his mouth ajar and a tear running down his cheek, he poked his head out from the branches and softly responding with one word: "here."

"Here," Zacchaeus said a second time as he cleared his throat and raised his hand. "Zacchaeus, come on down from there," said Jesus, "I'd like to stay at your place tonight." At the end of this story, Zacchaeus repented of his evil ways, vowed to repay everyone he's defrauded – ten times over and Jesus responded by saying: "Today, salvation has come to this house."

Friends, regardless of how undeserving or unworthy we feel, it's God who, in Jesus Christ, takes the initiative to come after us...seek us out – even when we are lost; even when we don't want to be found, and calls us by name. All the while waiting to hear one simple word from us: "here."

So "here" is a prayer that can be prayed, not just in the morning but throughout the day. For example, we can pray that simple prayer when, like Zacchaeus, we've made a mess of things or when we are struggling with guilt, embarrassment or even self-loathing. All we need to do is prayer: "here" and we are reminded that the God who accepts us is with us.

Or we can pray that simple prayer when we are in one of our typical multi-tasking, over-programmed days and we realize that our Lord hasn't been on our radar screen since 5:45am. All we need to do is stop and prayer: "here" and we are suddenly and joyfully brought back into the presence of our loving and living Lord.

When we pray "here" throughout the day, we are making ordinary moments, sacred moments and learning the practice of living in God's presence. (Question #3) <u>Think about it: By praying one simple word a few times a day, your relationship with our living lord can be completely renewed</u>. Do that long enough and your life will never be the same AND...you'll never feel like you're whistling in the dark.

EIGHT WORDS TO PRAY EVERY DAY: CORRESPONDING STUDY GUIDE

Below you will find the study guide for week I of: <u>Eight Words To Pray Every Day</u>. As you can see, I have put three sub-headings into the study guide that highlight our three-fold mission statement at the Bridge Presbyterian Church. Those sub-headings also serve to provide time and space for the small group to enjoy fellowship; prayer; Bible study; and mission. Also, note that I always provide more questions than needed and let the facilitators guide the conversation.

THE FIRST WORD: HERE

CONNECTING WITH GOD'S PEOPLE

Getting to Know Each Other:

Welcome to Week I of Sermon-Based Small Groups @ the Bridge!

Thank you for participating in the Eight Words to Pray Series. Because it's Week I, introductions are in order. Share your name; where you live; and what brought you to Leland area with the group?

CONNECTING WITH GOD'S PASSION

Digging Deeper

1. What insight, principle, or observation from this weekend's message did you find to be most helpful, eye-opening, or troubling? Explain.

2. What are some of the words that you think might be part of this sermon series and why? What words do you find yourself saying during the week that could become one-word prayers?

3. I (Doug) think much of religion today is superficial and doesn't help us find the presence of the Lord in our life or in the world. Do you agree or disagree? Why? What are the biggest challenges associated with experiencing the presence of the Lord in daily life?

4. The first word to pray every single day is the word *here*. When and how do you use the word *here*? How did Doug suggest that you pray this word? How might praying this word change your relationship with the Lord?

5. **Read I Samuel 16: 1- 13**. What do you learn about God in this passage? What do you learn about who and how God calls people into a relationship with God? Why do we have to wait until the very end of this passage to learn the name of the uninvited, unnoticed boy who becomes God's anointed? How does the fact that God knows your name impact your relationship with the Lord?

6. **Read Genesis 3: 8-9 & Isaiah 6:8**: Why do you think God called Adam by name in this story? What was Adam/Eve running from? How does the word 'here' function as a prayer in the Isaiah passage?

7. **Read Luke 19: 1-10**: Recall with the group what you have learned about Zacchaeus. Why do you think he climbed the sycamore tree? How do you think Zacchaeus must have felt when Jesus called him by name and told him he was coming to stay at his house? How do you think all those well-meaning, religious folks gathered around Jesus felt when the Lord said he was staying at Zacchaeus' house?

8. How did Zacchaeus respond when the Lord showed up at his house (basically saying: "I'm here?") What moved Zacchaeus to respond the way he did? What did the Lord say about Zacchaeus' response in verse 10?

9. Choose one of the passages from this study: **I Samuel 16: 1-13; Gen. 3:8-9; Isaiah 6:8; Luke 19: 1-10** and briefly share with the group what you've learned about God and/or your relationship with God from that passage.

Life Application: **(meditate on these questions in your devotional life)**

1. Spend a few minutes asking yourself what it means for YOU to pray this simple word: here – at least once day to the Lord. What does it mean to YOU to affirm that you are present in the presence of God every day? Share your thoughts with the group.

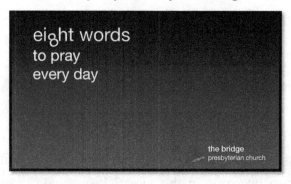

2. The point of the spiritual life is not to have dramatic spiritual experiences. What matters most – and is available to everyone – is daily, ordinary spiritual experiences. Ordinary spiritual experiences help us find and hold a sacred space in our life where we experience a vital connection with the living Lord. If able, share with the group ways you can pray 'here,' throughout the day as a way of staying connected to the Lord.

3. Use question #9 above in your devotional life this week.

CONNECTING WITH GOD'S PURPOSE

Gathering in worship and scattering on mission is the weekly rhythm at the Bridge. Each small group is asked to come up with a mission project that will help participants scatter on mission. Please begin prayerfully discussing how your small group is feeling led to scatter on mission. Each small group is asked to share their mission project with the congregation.

§

Here's a second example of how I create study guides from sermons. This is an example from a series I wrote titled: Letting God Fill Our Empty Places: Discovering Happiness In The Beatitudes. Below you will read a brief description of the series that I wrote for the congregation. Then, you'll be able to peruse an example of a sermon followed by the corresponding study guide.

LETTING GOD FILL OUR EMPTY PLACES: DESCRIPTION OF THE SERIES

This is the second example of how I create buzz and interest around the sermon series. As you can see, I created a sermon series icon that we used in-house and on social media. Additionally, I crafted a description of the series to draw people into a deeper interaction with God's Word while also seeing how the series has personal application.

There is a term in the advertising world called emotional branding which describes the emotional connection between products and consumers. Emotional branding provides consumers with meaning in life and, as one ad expert said: *"fills the empty places that civic institutions like schools and churches once did."* I'm convinced there is an empty place in every human soul and much of life is spent trying to fill that emptiness. This life-long quest to fill that empty place is called the pursuit of happiness. Unfortunately, no amount of happiness can fill the emptiness in our soul. Only a relationship with Jesus Christ can do that.

In the fifth chapter of the gospel of Matthew there are a series of seven short verses referred to as The Beatitudes. Each begins with the word *blessed*. The word *blessed* in the original language of the bible is *'makarios'* which (surprisingly) can be translated *happy*. Our Lord wants us to be happy, just not to pursue happiness as a goal. When our goals in life are shaped by the Beatitudes we find our empty places being filled by the Lord and...(you guessed it) happiness will happen.

Jesus teaches us in The Beatitudes that happiness waits for those who get busy doing God's will on earth. Echoing John Lennon we might say that happiness happens when we are busy making other plans. The other plans Jesus invites us to engage in are found in The Beatitudes. When our goals in life is shaped by The Beatitudes we will find our empty places being filled by the Lord and...(you guessed it) happiness will happen.

LETTING GOD FILL OUR EMPTY PLACES: SERMON EXAMPLE

Here is a sermon from: <u>Letting God Fill Our Empty Places</u>. Again, I have kept the insertions where I call for a slide to be put up on the screen. You will also see where I have included specific questions in the body of the sermon that will find their way into the study guide.

Life, Liberty, and the Tragic Pursuit for Happiness
A Sermon Preached From the Pulpit of
The Bridge Presbyterian Church

"Blessed are…" **Matthew 5: 1 - 12, NRSV**

Have any of you met a person that DIDN'T want to be happy? Gretchen Rubin, author of the book The Happiness Project writes: "Some people think that wanting to be happier is a selfish, self-absorbed goal – but I disagree. Robert Louis Stevenson got it right: 'There is no duty we so much underrate as the duty of being happy'."

Rubin points out that: "research shows that happy people are more altruistic, more productive, more helpful, more likeable, more creative, more resilient, more interested in the problems of others, friendlier, and healthier."[38]

Little wonder, then, that we treat happiness like some sort of deity. There is an uncritical, almost fanatical devotion to this idol. The way I hear people talk about happiness; you'd think that happiness is a god to be worshiped.

I remember an Elder at a previous church say to me: "I'm done with this job! I need to find something that makes me happy – even if it's only half the salary." Frequently, I hear parents say something like: "I think the guy is a bum but my daughter is in love with him. I'm cool if they get married as long as they are happy."

You want to know how important happiness is becoming? Happiness is now part of the equation in determining economic progress. Former Federal Reserve chairman, Ben Bernanke said that gauging happiness can be as important for measuring economic progress as the inflation or unemployment rates.[39] In fact, happiness is more than a goal…it's an inalienable right. We Americans are taught that we are entitled to happiness.

The wicked little irony about happiness, however, is that we are not very good at finding. Research tells us that we are poor at 1) predicting,

38   Gretchen Rubin, The Happiness Project http://happiness-project.com/
39   Christopher, S. Rugaber, "Ben Bernanke Has A Question for You: Are you Happy," *NBCNews.com*, August 10, 2012, http://economywatch.nbcnews.com/_news/2012/08/06/13148811-ben-bernanke-has-a-question-for-you-are-you-happy?lite

pursuing and practicing our own happiness.

(Slide #2) To help make my point, (Question #1) <u>let's look at the series of true/false questions I asked you earlier</u>. True or False?

___I would be happier if I made more money, found the perfect mate, lost 10 pounds or moved to a new house.

___Happiness is genetic. You can't change how happy you are any more than you can change how tall you are.

___Success brings happiness.

Answers: False, false and false.[40]

Now let's look at why this is so. (Slide # 3) The first point we need to understand about happiness is this: We're not good at practicing our own happiness because we think happiness is, largely, out of our control. Specifically, we think our happiness is either a product of our circumstances (I'd be happy if I had more money or the perfect mate) or our genetics. Those assumptions are both wrong!

Research tells us that only about 10% of our happiness is circumstantial. One study determined that those on the Forbes 100 list in 1995 were only slightly happier than the American public as a whole. In another 1978 study a group of researchers determined that 22 lottery winners were no happier than a control group. Similarly, researchers conducted a study of 29 people who'd recently become paraplegic or quadriplegic. It turned out the victims of these accidents reported no more unhappy moments than a control group.[41]

(Slide #4) Increasingly, there is consensus in the scholarly community that happiness is 50% genetic, 10% circumstantial and 40% intentional.[42]

---

40   Marnell Jameson, "C'Mon Get Happy," *LA Times*, September 8, 2008. Preachers are infatuated with alliterating sermon points. This survey that Jameson uses at the beginning of the article is a wonderful way to introduce a discussion of why humans are not good at predicting, pursuing or practicing happiness.

41   This came from a study by Philip Brickman cited in "Some Dark Thoughts on Happiness," by Deborah Senior, *New York Magazine*, July 17, 2006. https://nymag.com/news/features/17573/

42   Jameson, *C'Mon Get Happy*, 2008.

In reality, the circumstances of life have far less of an impact on our happiness than we think. So, we need to re-think the idea that our boss or our spouse or our bank account or our health is what is preventing us from being happier.

In addition to not practicing happiness very well, we're not very good at predicting what will make us happy. Daniel Gilbert wrote a fascinating book called <u>Stumbling on Happiness</u>. The books contention is that we have a limited capacity to remember what made us happy and we are poor at imagining our future happiness. Thus, we don't do a good job predicting what will make us happy.

(Slide #5) Gilbert writes: "We insist on steering our boats (down the river of time) because we think we have a pretty good idea of where we should go, but the truth is that much of our steering is in vain – not because the boat won't respond, and not because we can't find our destination, but because the future is fundamentally different than it appears."[43] In short, we are terrible predictors of future happiness.

So, part of what I'm arguing for this morning is that while happiness is like the Holy Grail for many Americans, we're terrible at practicing, predicting and (most importantly) pursuing our happiness. Dr. Ed Diener, who has written a book titled: <u>Happiness: Unlocking the Secrets to Psychological Health</u>, insightfully states: "If you have no goal other than your personal happiness, you'll never achieve it. If you want to be happy, pursue something else vigorously and happiness will catch up with you."[44]

In our time, perhaps, nobody has helped us re-think the pursuit of happiness better than Psychiatrist and concentration camp survivor Victor Frankl. Through the horrors of Auschwitz Frankl came to realize the futility of a life lived in pursuit of happiness. His words about <u>happiness and</u> success are, perhaps, the most insightful to us in our

43   Gilbert, Daniel, <u>Stumbling on Happiness</u>, (New York: Vantage Books, 2005), p 25.
44   Diener, Ed, "Happiness: Unlocking the Mysteries of Psychological Wealth," in Jameson, Marnell, C'Mon Get Happy, <u>LA Times</u>, September 8, 2008.

search for happiness.

(Slide # 6) Frankl says: "Don't aim at success. The more you aim at it and make it a target, the more you are going to miss it. For success, like happiness, cannot be pursued; it must ensue, and it only does so as the unintended side effect of one's personal dedication to a cause greater than oneself or as the by-product of one's surrender to a person other than oneself. Happiness must happen, and the same holds for success: you have to let it happen by not caring about it."[45]

Or, as Ed Diener points out, "What happiness isn't, is getting everything right in your life. A man might think, 'If I get the right education, the right job and the right wife, I'll be happy.' But that's not how it works. For instance, once basic needs are met, the effects of income on happiness get smaller and smaller. That's because happiness lies in the way you live and look at the world."[46]

So our American pursuit happiness is ironic. On one hand it is an obsession...even an entitlement, yet we are not very good at predicting, practicing or pursuing the very thing we seem obsessed with. (Question #2) <u>What sort of happiness are you pursuing</u>?

Happiness, it appears, is something hidden, a bit elusive, something that is a gift received by NOT pursuing it. If we want to discover happiness in our lifetime, I think we need to begin looking at our self and our world through a different lens.

Jesus provides us with such a lens and it's found in the fifth chapter of Matthew. Turn with me to Matthew 5: 1 – 12. As you can see embedded within these 12 verses, we find a litany of 9 verses that begin with the word (what) *blessed*.

The Greek word for *blessed* is *makarios* which, as you probably have guessed, has a wide range of meaning. Scholars have translated this <u>word as follows</u>: fortunate, joyful, congratulations, God cares about

---

45   Frankl, Victor, <u>Man's Search for Meaning</u>, (Boston, Beacon Press, 1959).

46   Diener, Ed, "Happiness: Unlocking the Mysteries of Psychological Wealth," in James-on, Marnell, C'Mon Get Happy, LA Times, September 8, 2008.

you, I am on your side. But most scholars acknowledge that when Jesus said to the crowd "blessed are you," he was saying something about happiness.

For the next 8 weeks I'm going to translate the word *makarios* as happy. But I want to nuance this translation because I think the type of happiness that Jesus promises in these beatitudes has an elusive quality about it.

Similar to what we are learning from contemporary research the type of happiness promised in Matthew 5 is not a happiness we can plan, predict or pursue. It's a happiness that ensues when we pursue God and God's will for our life. (Question #3) <u>Where and how are you pursuing God's will for your life, right now</u>?

(Slide #7) Years ago John Lennon famously said: "Life is what happens while you are busy making other plans." I think what Jesus is saying in these beatitudes is very similar. I think our Lord is saying that happiness is what happens while you are busy making other plans. And what sort of plans might Jesus be referring to? The answer is found in these series of sentences which begin with the word 'blessed.'

You know all those empty places in your life you are trying to fill by pursuing happiness? Try this instead.

LETTING GOD FILL OUR EMPTY PLACES: CORRESPONDING STUDY GUIDE

Below you will find the study guide corresponding to the sermon. The pattern for the study guide is much the same as the one you viewed above. I have put three sub-headings into the study guide that highlights our three-fold mission statement at the Bridge Presbyterian Church. Those sub-headings also serve to provide time and space for the small group to enjoy fellowship; prayer; Bible study; and mission. Also, note that I always provide more questions than needed and let the facilitators guide the conversation.

LIFE, LIBERTY AND THE TRAGIC PURSUIT OF HAPPINESS

CONNECTING WITH GOD'S PEOPLE

Getting to Know Each Other:

Welcome to Week III of Sermon-Based Small Groups @ the Bridge! Go around the room, introduce yourself and share with the group one thing that consistently makes you happy.

CONNECTING WITH GOD'S PASSION

Digging Deeper

1. What insight, principle, or observation from this weekend's message did you find to be most helpful, eye-opening, or troubling? Explain

2. Discuss with the group how you answered these three questions, (remember that studies show the correct answers to be false, false and false).

3. ___ I would be happier if I made more money, found the perfect mate, lost 10 pounds or moved to a new house.

   ___ Happiness is genetic. You can't change how happy you are any more than you can change how tall you are.

   ___ Success brings happiness

4. What do you make of this research on happiness? How does this research relate to the above three questions? Discuss what you

think the key is to sustaining happiness in life.

5. **Read Matthew 5: 1 – 12**: Share with the group your initial questions, observations and comments about these verses. Verses 2 – 12 are referred to as the Beatitudes. Looking closely at the beatitudes, discuss the following questions: Which of the 9 Beatitudes is easiest for you to understand? Why? Which of the 9 Beatitudes is hardest to figure out? Why? Which Beatitude do you most connect with? Why? If possible, have someone note the questions the group wants answered and send them to Doug.

6. If we substitute the word 'blessed' with the word 'happy'[47] then what do you think Jesus is saying about the path to discovering happiness in the Beatitudes? **Read Psalm 1:1-3; Luke 11:28; Rev 22:7**. What do these passages say about God's path toward discovering happiness? How does the Jesus path toward happiness differ from our cultural understanding of happiness?

Personal Application (For use in your devotional time and small group discussion)

*   Continue to study the passages above on your own asking yourself: What do these passages tell me about God's plan to discover happiness? What kind of happiness does God want us to experience? How are you experiencing that happiness right now?

*   How does this statement relate to Jesus' path to happiness in Matthew 5? *"If you have no goal other than your personal happiness, you'll never achieve it. If you want to be happy, pursue something else vigorously and happiness will catch up*

---

47   The Greek word for *'blessed'* is *'makarios'* which, as you probably have guessed, has a wide range of meaning. Scholars have translated this word as follows: *'fortunate,' 'joyful,' 'congratulations,' 'God cares about you,' 'I am on your side.'* But most scholars acknowledge that when Jesus said to the crowd *'blessed are you'* he was saying something about happiness.

with you."[48]

- What one thing can you do to strengthen your relationship with

the Lord that will lead to more happiness?

- Here's a suggested prayer for your devotional life this week based on the premise that true happiness is discovered by doing God's will: Not what I want, but what you want, O God. Guard me from all temptations that use you to satisfy my appetites. What I want mostly is to acquire new appetites, a hunger for righteousness that will be satisfied by your Word. Amen

CONNECTING WITH GOD'S PURPOSE

If you've chosen a mission coordinator, have her or him loop back with Doug and explain the mission your group has selected.

Begin thinking about someone(s) who can share what your group is doing with the church in worship.

---

48 The Greek word for 'blessed' is 'makarios' which, as you probably have guessed, has a wide range of meaning. Scholars have translated this word as follows: 'fortunate,' 'joyful,' 'congratulations,' 'God cares about you,' 'I am on your side.' But most scholars acknowledge that when Jesus said to the crowd 'blessed are you' he was saying something about happiness.

CHAPTER FIVE

CONNECTING MISSIONAL SERMON-BASED SMALL GROUPS TO GOD'S MISSION FOR YOUR CHURCH

THINGS NEED TO CHANGE

It's Tuesday morning and you are in your pastor's study looking over the week that lies ahead. The first thing you need to do is prepare for yet another predictable staff meeting. You're wondering how you are going to possibly motivate the part-time music director who is disgruntled over lack of commitment shown by the choir. Additionally, you dread the constant tension between the very traditional church administrative assistant and the very innovative, yet young, part-time youth director.

You just learned that you no longer possess that three-hour block of time in the afternoon that you had carved out to work on the sermon. Instead you will be meeting with two dedicated but weary leaders in your congregation. They want to share with you their concerns about the upcoming Habitat for Humanity work day. It seems that the participation has been steadily decreasing over the past two years to the point where they are wondering if it's time to pull the plug on the church's partnership with Habitat.

Wednesday's schedule looks much like Tuesday's schedule. The day begins early with the morning Rotary Club meeting where you will try your best to come up with, yet, another creative opening prayer while at the same time keeping the prayer, "short and sweet" as the Rotary President habitually reminds you. The rest of the morning you are going to begin preparing for the fall Christian education rally with that innovative youth minister and the volunteer Sunday School superintendent who has repeatedly said to you she needs to step down at the end of the year.

The Christian education theme for this year is: <u>What's New in Christian Formation</u>, which you openly admit lacks the appeal needed to lure anyone back into the old, tired Sunday school that has been on life-support for the past 6 years. Then, there is the afternoon meeting with the fellowship committee elder, where the two of you will discuss what is needed to spice up the coffee hours held after worship every third Sunday.

It's a busy week, but at least you have Thursday to work on the Sunday sermon. Although, after six-years of preaching at your current congregation, you've begun wondering if your preaching is really shaping the lives of the people in the pews or inspiring change in the neighborhoods around your church.

At some point in your week you will wonder out loud when was the last time you were so excited about your calling that you beat the alarm clock getting out of bed. Does any of this sound familiar? Is your weekly rhythm, that once felt so invigorating, turning into a grind? Do you and the leaders of your church feel stuck, or worse yet, trapped? If so, maybe it's time to consider re-organizing your congregation around a vision of missional sermon-based small groups.

The shift can help you and your congregation realize your dream of passionately engaging in mission and outreach in the neighborhoods around your congregation...without you having to lead the charge! Missional sermon-based small groups can become the catalyst breathing new life into your congregation while also creating a passion to love and serve your neighbors in the name of Jesus.

Guess what! You're not the only one feeling hungry for a new way of doing and being church. So are those weary leaders in charge of the local Habitat project. So is that disgruntled part-time director of music. So is the Rotary President. So is that burnt-out educator and that innovative youth director and the fellowship elder.

It should come as no surprise to you that the very people who show up every Sunday to worship God are eager for new life and renewed spiritual passion. Believe it or not, so are the people in your neighborhood who you've never met and who may not realize how spiritually hungry they truly are. Most importantly, so is our risen, reigning and active Lord who longs for your congregation to experience the renewed joy of ministry in your neighborhood.

If you are at the point where you feel like things absolutely, positively, unquestionably need to change, then you are ready to begin making the shift to missional sermon-based small groups. If the congregation you are part of feels stuck, stale, bored and in a spiritual rut, then you ready to begin making the shift to missional sermon-based small groups. Are you ready for something new that is time-tested, easy to implement and potentially game-changing?

In the previous chapters, I outlined a process that will guide you (and the team you gather) toward successfully launching missional sermon-based small groups within your congregation. If you use the process or adapt it to your context, you will likely be able to successfully launch a small-group ministry within a year.

However, there is one more consideration you and your small group team should ponder before starting on your journey toward missional sermon-based small groups. That consideration has to do with the 'big-picture.' A wholesale, congregation-wide shift to missional sermon-based small groups begins at the thirty-thousand-foot level. Before you begin tinkering with changes to Sunday worship or revamp how your congregation understands and embodies mission in your community, consider taking a fresh look at the big picture. Re-examining the big picture begins with a discussion of how your congregation understands its vocation.

Do the members of your church have a clear and compelling understanding of what's most important in your congregation? Can they quickly and effortlessly explain what the mission of your church is all about? Does your church possess a mission or vision statement that is known and easily embodied? Most importantly, is that statement consistent with a vision for missional sermon-based small groups?

Whether or not you have a relevant, engaging and faithful mission or vision statement, this conversation is very important...maybe essential. Please don't gloss over this portion of the book. Everything else I have shared in this book rests on the foundation of developing a compelling, easily-understood mission statement that aligns four essential parts of your church: 1) Sunday worship; 2) local mission outreach; 3) Christian formation and 4) congregational fellowship.

Central to my vision of missional sermon-based small groups is the integration of worship, mission, discipleship and fellowship. When these four essential parts of your church are integrated within a sermon-based small group ministry, new life and vitality will flourish and, wait for it...your workload will decrease while your work-joy will increase.

However, without a mission statement that brings worship, mission, discipleship and fellowship into alignment, your efforts to make the shift to missional sermon-based small groups will, likely, be twice as hard to complete and twice as easy to abandon.

As I stated in chapter one, the shift to missional sermon-based small groups begins with God's calling to join Jesus in our Lord's ministry of extending the Kingdom of God to your neighborhood. Unless your congregation has a sense of call to join Jesus on mission in your neighborhood, developing an effective, long-lasting missional sermon-based small group ministry will be an uphill battle.

But here's the good news! Your congregation already possesses that desire to join Jesus on mission in your community – even if they don't realize it. Our Lord has already planted that desire within your congregation. As the Pastor (or lay leader) your job is to get people in touch with what Jesus is already doing internally to create a missional passion in your church.

Consider this: For over two years your congregation has likely been forced to make extraordinary, unprecedented changes due to the pandemic. Now, as the pandemic loosens its grip on the world, your congregation has changed. They may not want to admit it and they may long to return to *the way things used to be.* But everyone who has remained faithful to your congregation's mission and ministry has been changed because of the pandemic.

This may well be the ideal time to invite the congregation to recover its outward focus and join Jesus in our Lord's work in the community around your church. Underneath the anxiety expressed in statements like: "We really need to grow our church," and "Will our congregation ever recover and return to normal," lies the opportunity for you to redirect that anxiety by pointing your congregation toward their God-given calling to be a blessing, the tangible touch of God in your local community.

If you feel the first step toward developing missional sermon-based small groups is to help your congregation rediscover their missional passion, then here are some suggestions you can try that will help your church recover their identity as God's called and sent people.

IDEAS TO HELP YOUR CONGREGATION
REDISCOVER THEIR MISSIONAL PASSION

If you are a pastor reading this book, then consider creating a series of sermons that point your worshiping community to God's desire to be a blessing in your community. There are so many creative options in Scripture that will help your congregation recover their identity as God's called and sent people.

1. One option is the book of Jonah – a reluctant missionary. A second option is a journey through the book of Acts.

2. Gather a group of interested people (that could possibly become your Circle of Ten) by inviting them to read and discuss a book that will inspire them to follow Jesus into the local neighborhoods. I would suggest the book Tangible Kingdom[49] by Halter and Smay along with the Tangible Kingdom Primer.[50]

Another book that has been, for many, a launching pad to recover the church's missional identity is Missional Church[51] by Darrell Guder et al. This book is theologically loaded and may not be as accessible for some folks.

Another suggestion for a reading group is the book Shaped By God's Heart: The Passion and Practices of Missional Churches by Milfred Manatrea.[52] One final suggestion is the book SHIFT: Three Big Moves For The 21st Century Church by Mark Tidsworth.[53]

3. A third idea to help your congregation recover their missional passion is to host a mission rally that highlights all the local mission partnerships your church has with local mission agencies. Back in the day, some churches might call this the annual missions fair. But it is a

---

49 Halter & Smay, *The Tangible Kingdom*.
50 Halter & Smay, *The Tangible Kingdom Primer*.
51 Milfred Manatrea, *Shaped By God's Heart: The Passion and Practices of Missional Churches*, (Hoboken, Jossey Bass, 2010).
52 Guder, *Missional Church*.
53 Tidsworth, *Shift*.

great way to help the congregation see and learn about the long-standing partnerships with local mission organization. Invite a representative from each agency your church supports to speak in worship on the Sunday of your mission rally. Encourage each of your churches mission partners to set up a kiosk in your gathering area to help interpret their ministry to the congregation.

4. Yet, another idea to increase your congregational awareness of what the Lord is already at work doing in your church is to develop the habit of having your congregation tell stories about how they have been blessed, inspired, changed by being on mission with Jesus. Begin and end every committee or team meeting by inviting folks to share their stories. Invite folks to share their stories in worship is another way to hear what Jesus is doing to grow missional passion.

If that sounds like too big of a step, begin by training your staff and leadership team to listen for stories about how Jesus is at work in your congregation. The best way to do that is by sharing your stories with the staff and the leadership team. The above suggestions are but a handful of ideas you can use to start recovering your congregation's passion to be on mission with Jesus in your neighborhood.

CRAFTING A COMPELLING, MISSIONAL MISSION STATEMENT

What I want to talk about for the remainder of this chapter is how to craft a winsome, compelling and faithful mission statement that will inspire members of your congregation to join Jesus in our Lord's ministry of extending the Kingdom of God in your neighborhood. A collaboratively crafted and thoroughly embraced mission statement inviting your congregation to be the church to its neighbors is the glue that binds worship, mission, discipleship and fellowship together. It's the thread that weaves together the components of a successful sermon-based small group ministry.

Ultimately, that mission statement will need to be aligned with how you and your small group planning team (or Circle of Ten) intend to integrate worship, small groups, mission and fellowship within your congregation. Ahead you will hear how I crafted the mission statement at the Bridge Presbyterian Church followed by a practical guide for how you can do this work in your context.

Once this mission statement has been crafted (hopefully by a planning team you or the congregation have selected and adopted by your church leaders and the congregation, then will you be ready to launch your missional sermon-based small group ministry in your church. But this shift to missional sermon-based small groups doesn't begin with a planning team or the churches leadership team. Nor does it begin in corporate worship or in a Christian education planning retreat. The shift begins in the neighborhoods around your church as you listen to the very people our Lord is calling you to bear witness to God's love in Jesus Christ.

HOW I CREATED OUR MISSION STATEMENT: LISTENING TO THE NEEDS IN THE NEIGHBORHOOD

As I share the story of how I crafted the initial mission statement for what became the Bridge Presbyterian Church, I do so with the keen recognition that my story is just that: My story. Your story and your mission statement will be different and unique. Thanks be to God! My goal in sharing my story with you is to fire your imagination; inspire you to dream bold dreams and nudge you and your church leaders to begin asking what's next for our congregation?

Sometimes when I hear how the Holy Spirit is working in a different church or through a different pastor, it sets my imagination on fire not to replicate what I've learned but to adapt what I've learned to my environment. Learning how the Holy Spirit is leading in a very different context helps me think creatively about new ways to be a faithful and relevant leader in my context.

So, my hope is that by sharing the story of how I developed a mission statement and aligned my system of missional sermon-based small groups around that mission statement, I trust you will be inspired to think and act creativity and imaginatively as you are led by the Spirit of the living God.

Although my story was born out of my experience as a church planter, please don't let that discourage you. If you're eager for change and feel the Holy Spirit is calling you to make the shift to missional sermon-based small groups, there's no reason you can't reproduce in your own unique way, what the Holy Spirit did in my context.

Prior to launching the Bridge Presbyterian Church, I felt deeply called to create an internal DNA that would support and sustain a church-wide emphasis on missional sermon based small groups. While I wasn't quite sure how to develop and implement sermon-based small groups, I knew that whatever type of small group ministry the Lord would grow in the future new church, the focus would have to be on learning what Jesus was already doing in the neighborhoods of the city.

I arrived in Leland, North Carolina in Nov 2013 intent on launching a new Presbyterian Church that would make a difference in the neighborhood. My first priority was to understand my neighbors and my neighborhood. I found myself going to just about any public place in the city with the hope of meeting people and listening to their joys and concerns about living in the community I was called to serve.

Within the first few weeks of my arrival, I made a practice of going to the local McDonalds, buying breakfast and attempting to engage strangers about my desire to launch a new Presbyterian Church. By the way, if you are a church planter or feeling called to plant a new church, please don't do this! Trust me, nobody wants to talk about theology, Jesus or new churches at 7:30am while they are munching on an Egg McMuffin and trying to read the morning headlines on their cell phone.

Early one morning, while sitting alone at McDonalds, I began wondering if the first and most important step needed to create a congregation-wide system of missional sermon-based small groups was to craft an easy-to-understand mission statement that reflected the needs of the neighborhood and then align the small groups around that mission statement.

But how would I take on such an exciting but daunting challenge? Over time and with much prayer, I realized that the starting point was to answer these three foundational questions:

1. Who is my neighbor?
2. What's up in my neighborhood?
3. How can I craft a mission statement based on what I'm learning about my neighborhood?

I used the raw data I learned from asking these questions to cobble together an initial mission statement. Then I began exploring imaginative, creative ways to align my initial mission statement with a congregation-wide system of missional sermon-based small groups. The ultimate aim was to create a mission statement that would inspire those who joined the future church be the church to our neighbors.

By necessity, I was forced to seek answers to the above three questions on my own Unlike most of my readers, I didn't yet have a congregation to join me this important, initial task. If you decide to take on the task of creating a mission statement, you will undoubtedly have the benefit of inviting folks from your congregation to form a team to join you in this exciting journey.

Returning to my story, in addition to my ill-fated attempts at chatting people up at the McDonalds, I also joined organizations like the Leland-area Newcomers and the local Chamber of Commerce. I'm sure there are a ton of local ministries and civic organizations that will help you grow deep connections in your community while learning about the challenges, pain and needs of your neighbors.

While I was able to listen and learn from people as a result of joining local organizations and engaging people in local restaurants, I was also blessed to inherit 8 – 10 fellow Presbyterians who lived in the Leland area, but attended Presbyterian Churches across the Cape Fear River in downtown Wilmington, N.C. They became what I referred to in chapter 2 as my Circle of Ten.[54] Developing relationships with the Circle of Ten proved to be pure gold.

While the Circle of Ten made it clear to me that they were happy in their current churches and had no intention on joining the soon-to-be emerging new congregation, nonetheless, they were happy to help me.

The first thing we agreed upon was to meet weekly in the local barbeque restaurant. Like most Christians I know, our gatherings accomplished more because we were sitting around a table eating good barbeque. Surely that's not just a 'Presbyterian thing,' is it?

Two important developments emerged from these very initial, informal gathering. One, I could see the Holy Spirit working in the lives of these people, slowly, deliberately creating in some of that Circle of Ten a passion to help launch the future new church. Secondly, the group decided our efforts to launch a new church would benefit by organizing bi-monthly Meet & Greets in their homes.

---

54   In this chapter the Circle of Ten is the term I used to describe the first group of interested seekers who helped to launch the new church I currently serve. I've discussed the Circle of Ten in detail in chapter two. A similar term is a small group planning team. In this chapter, I will use the language of the Circle of Ten and the small group planning team synonymously to refer to the team of people the Lord raises up to help you make the shift to missional sermon-based small groups.

The idea behind our Meet & Greets was simple. We would gather interested people (typically the friends and neighbors of The Circle of Ten) together in a non-threatening way and do life together. Our Meet & Greets were held in living rooms and kitchens of the Circle of Ten. They were held on Sundays from four until six pm. Everyone was to bring an appetizer; a beverage of choice and a friend or two. The Circle of Ten began inviting friends and neighbors.

Discussion Questions:

1. What civic organizations or local ministries could you join that would help you learn more about your neighbors?

2. Who could be your Circle of Ten? Can you identify up to ten people in your congregation who would be eager to join you on this journey to discover where the Lord is at work in your neighborhood?

3. I used Meet & Greets to listen and learn about the neighborhood in which I was planting a church. What vehicle could you and your Circle of Ten use to listen and learn about your neighborhood?

I spent the next six months listening and learning about my neighbors and my neighborhoods at those Meet & Greets. Among the things I learned, two of my initial hunches were confirmed. When I took the call to be Organizing Pastor, I was told that Brunswick Co. NC is the fastest growing county in the state and among the top 50 fastest growing counties in US. So, the first thing I learned was that most folks in my neighborhood were relatively new and looking to connect with other people. (Sometimes that which is most obvious is also what is most needed).

Listening to people at the Meet & Greets, I learned that nobody was from Brunswick Co., NC. Because of that, the neighbors in my neighborhood were struggling with loneliness and isolation. I witnessed this isolation every morning while walking my dog through the neighborhood where my wife and I were renting a home.

Every morning I walk past once home after another. Each home shared similar characteristics. Every home had a six-foot privacy fence around their back yard. The front drapes of every home were drawn. The doors and windows shut. The garage door closed. And, except the occasional sound of a car driving down the road, I walked my dog in utter silence.

Part of the rhythm of life in that neighborhood was learning to deal with isolation. Yet, as I met and listened to neighbors at our Meet and Greets, I learned they possessed a genuine desire to meet others in their neighborhoods. The first discovery I made was that the neighbors in my neighborhoods had a felt need to connect with other people. Even though they appeared to be very busy, nonetheless, they felt isolated, alone and they longed for an authentic connection to other neighbors.

This loneliness was caused, in part, by the rapid growth in Brunswick Co. This growth was fueled by the development of high-end, amenity-rich planned communities. These planned communities were marketing themselves up and down the east coast. This led to my second insight. A majority of new neighbors were transplanted northerners. Additionally, I discovered that most of the transplants were also retirees.

The second largest demographic in our neighborhoods were millennials who were attracted to a relatively low cost of living in

Leland as compared to the higher cost of living in Wilmington metro area. Both the retirees and the millennials arrived in Leland asking the same question but from two very different perspectives. They were both searching for ways to make meaning in life.

Author Daniel Pink helped me to articulate what I was learning about the newly retired boomers and the millennials. In his book: Drive: The Surprising Truth About What Motivates Us, Pink writes: *"In 2006, the first members of the baby-boom generation began turning sixty. When people reach the Big 60, they typically move through a three-stage reaction. In the first stage, they ask: 'How in the heck did I get to be sixty?' When people hit sixty, they are often surprised and slightly alarmed. They tally their regrets and realize that Mick Jagger was right: 'you can't always get what you want.'*

But then the second stage kicks in. In the not-so-distant past, turning sixty meant you were old. Not so anymore. According to the UN data, a sixty-year-old American man can expect to live for another twenty-plus years; and a sixty-year-old woman can expect to be around for over a quarter century. As you might expect, this realization brings with it a certain relief: "I've got a couple more decades.

This relief is followed, almost immediately, by the third stage: 60-year-old folks look back 25 years, realize how quickly time flew by and then ask the really important question: "When am I going to live my best life? When am I going to do something that really matters?"[55]

Truth is, it's not just people 60 and over who are looking for purpose in life. The generation birthed by Baby-Boomers called the Millennials, or the Echo Boomers are asking the same question. This generation does not rate money as the most important form of compensation.

Instead, among the most important factors in life is: *"the ability to give back to society through work."* A 2011 report conducted by Harris Interactive, found that the No. 1 factor that young adults ages 21 to 31

---

55   Daniel Pink, *Drive: The Surprising Truth About What Motivates Us.* (New York: Penguin Group: 2011), 129-130.

wanted in a successful career was a sense of meaning.[56]

Author Daniel Pink sums it up best when he writes: *"From the moment that human beings first stared into the sky, contemplated their place in the universe, and tried to create something that bettered the world and outlasted their lives, we have been purpose seekers."*[57]

Virtually every conversation I had with my neighbors, whether they were 32 years old or 72 years old confirmed what Pink was claiming in his book. The second insight I gleaned from listening to my neighbors was that the people in my neighborhoods longed to make meaning in life. They had a felt need to connect with a purpose in life.

Our bi-monthly Meet and Greets were attracting new and interested seekers. Within three months, our Meet and Greets grew from 10 to around 35 people and most were genuinely interested in getting involved with God's mission to launch a new church.

As more and more folks got involved in our Meet and Greets, they grew comfortable sharing their joys and struggles with me. What I discovered was something of a dichotomy. On the one hand, most people would tell me that they were 'living the dream!' And by all accounts, living in Leland can look and feel like living the dream.

Leland North Carolina is about twenty minutes from any one of a number of awesome beaches. To live in Leland is to live the coastal lifestyle. Additionally, the transplants who relocated from somewhere up north enjoyed lower taxes, larger, more luxurious homes, a warmer, more pleasant climate, and an emerging community filled with great restaurants, shops and outstanding health care.

So, on one hand, my neighbors were 'living the dream.' Yet, they repeatedly told me that even with all the wonderful blessing that came with living on the coast, it didn't quite seem to be enough. My new neighbors were looking for something more; something better,

56   Emily Esfahani Smith and Jennifer L. Aaker, "Millennial Searchers," *New York Times*, Nov 30, 2013, Sunday Review.
57   Pink, *Drive*, 131.

something else.

I discovered that even though my neighbors felt like they were living the dream, there was an emptiness deep in their soul - a longing for transcendence. They had yet to discover the truth of Augustine's discovery, that *"my heart is restless until I find my rest in Thee."*[58]

The third insight I gained about the neighbors in my neighborhood was that they were getting in touch with an emptiness in their soul that God alone could fill. They were longing for a connection with the presence of God.

What emerged from those conversations with my new neighbors was an evolving mission statement for the new church I hoped to launch. That mission statement was based on the needs and longings I heard expressed by the neighbors in my neighborhood. I was becoming increasingly convinced that God was calling me to launch a new Presbyterian church committed to helping people make three important connections. The mission of this new church would be to help neighbors connect with God's people, passion and purpose for life.

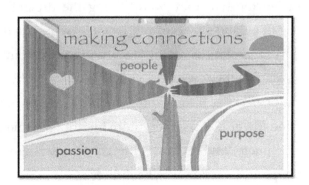

CREATING YOUR MISSION STATEMENT: THE NEEDS IN YOUR NEIGHBORHOOD

---

58   This is the famous passage from St. Augustine's *Confessions* (Lib 1,1-2,2.5,5: CSEL 33, 1-5) in which Saint Augustine states "You have made us for yourself, O Lord, and our heart is restless until it rests in you." It is also sometimes translated in the plural: "our hearts are restless until they rest in you."

Now that you've heard the story of my maiden voyage into my neighborhood and how the insights I gained from hundreds of conversations led to the development of a mission statement pictured above, I'm going take you through a similar process. The steps I took to get to know my neighbors in my neighborhood are the steps I'm going to take you through, with one notable exception.

The assumption we will make is that you are not a church planter struggling to develop a brand-new mission statement for a brand-new congregation. If you happen to be reading this book and you are a church planter, the process I'm about to layout will work just fine. But for most readers, the assumption is that you are connected to an existing congregation.

So, the steps I'm going to take you through consist of you asking and answering the following questions. You may choose to engage these questions by yourself (which I did by necessity) or with a group from your congregation (your <u>Circle of Ten</u>). Obviously, a group discussion has some distinct advantages over riding through these questions solo. Here are the 4 questions:

Question #1: Who Are Our Neighbors?

Question #2: What's Going on in Our Neighborhoods?

Question #3: What's Going on in Our Congregation?

Question #4: How Can We Connect the Patterns of Church with Neighborhood?

WHO ARE OUR NEIGHBORS?

It's a simple question that Jesus asked over and over. Who is your neighbor?[59] Are you able to describe the needs, fears, joys, concerns and struggles of the people who live in the neighborhoods around

---

59   Luke 10: 25 - 37

your church? Can your congregation articulate the factors that shape the individual and communal identity of those who live within three miles of your church parking lot? Can your congregation articulate the rhythm of life your neighbors embody?

In his extremely insightful book <u>Missional Church Groups: Becoming a Community that Makes a Difference</u>, author M Scott Boren dedicates chapter two to discussing the rhythms of everyday life. Boren writes: *"the place to begin is to understand how we live life today in the culture in which we live. We must grapple with what it means for people to do life, not in an ideal way, but in an everyday way. When we understand the rhythms of normal, everyday life that most of us live, then we can begin to see how the rhythms of Christ's bride begin to intersect with the rhythms of the culture."* [60]

The steps I take you through below reflect both Boren's vision of integrating the rhythms of everyday life and the rhythms of Christ's bride with my own, intuitive (Spirit-led) work in launching the missional sermon-based small groups that have been the backbone of our new church. I'm indebted to Scott Boren for helping to give language to my experience of launching a new church and the small group ministry that sustains that new church.

The first step toward understanding your neighbors is to develop a <u>Neighborhood Identity Diagram</u>. You can use this tool by yourself or, for better results, with the Circle of Ten that the Lord has raised up to join you in this work.

A <u>Neighborhood Identity Diagram</u> will help you and your team learn about the way your neighbors do life, what needs those women and men have and how the Lord is already at work in the lives of those people. The Neighborhood Identity Diagram and the example below are inspired by Randy Frazee and his book <u>Making Room for Life</u>.[61]

---

60   Boren, *Missional Small Groups*, location 238 of 1954
61   Randy Frazee, *Making Room for Life* (Grand Rapids: Zondervan, 2004). See also M Scott Boran, Missional Small Groups, Becoming A Community that Makes a Difference, location 261.

Let me offer an example of a <u>Neighborhood Identity Diagram</u> from the fictitious lives of Brent and Hillary Clark.

Brent is a 45-year-old bank manager at First Bank, a locally owned bank. Brent days are always busy. His goal is to rise by 5:30, get a three-mile jog and a shower done in time to help navigate his and Hillary's four children through breakfast and off to school. Brent and Hillary are parents to the two youngest children while Brent is the 'step-dad' to the older two children from Hillary's first marriage.

Hillary's teenaged kids have never quite accepted Brent as their 'step-dad,' which leads to tension and flash points in the family. Yet, all four children work hard in school and everyone except the youngest who has recently been diagnosed with dyslexia, are doing well.

Brent arrives at First Bank in time to open the doors for other employees. His work days are spent alternating between problem-solving; meeting with existing clients and developing business relationships within the community. Typically, Brent comes homes exhausted and the ongoing tension in the blended family causes him to retreat to his basement where he fiddles with his woodworking hobby.

Hillary is part-owner of a pet store specializing in products for dogs. Being a partial-owner of the store offers Hillary flexible hours and the chance to connect with her love of dogs. Having her and Brent's parents living locally is a big help as well because they each volunteer at the pet store. Finances are always tight which creates stress for Hillary and Brent and prevents the Clarks from taking fancy vacations. So, they focus instead on Friday evening happy hours with their two sets of friends, the Billing's and the Foster's.

Hillary is also active in the local Kiwanis Club and while she enjoys her involvement, she constantly feels guilty because the demands of parenting and owning a business prevent her from being more involved in club.

Let's look at the <u>Neighborhood Identity Diagram</u> to illustrate how Brent does life. All of the circles around Brent illustrate the different parts of his life that he must manage. He has a lot of people in his life, but no relationships of any depth. He even struggles to find time to be with his

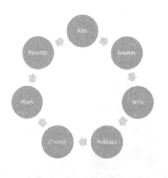

wife. Imagine Brent and Hillary live one block from your congregation. What are the patterns of life that Brent and Hillary follow? What do you think are their greatest needs? What are their greatest challenges? How might you shape ministry and outreach in a way that connects with the Brent and Hillary?

GROUP DISCUSSION: WHO ARE OUR NEIGHBORS?

Open your gathering with prayer, asking the Holy Spirit to bless your work and guide your conversations. You will likely need a dry erase board or some electronic way of displaying the answers your team comes up with. Begin by introducing the concept of a <u>Neighborhood Identity Diagram</u> by using the description above. Even after you use that description, there will be some initial confusion about what you are asking your team to do. Part of the reason is because this type of work, and these questions, may be very new to the people in your team. Push through and realize that as the team gets more comfortable with the material, the creativity and collaboration will increase.

Make your own <u>Neighborhood Identity Diagram.</u>
- What patterns do you see?
- What are your most important connections in life? How well are you sustaining those connections?
- What spiritual needs do you see emerging? What are the greatest challenges that arise from your daily living?
- Come up with **five words** to describe your Life Rhythm.

In a small group – Think about some of your neighbors/work colleagues/friends. Take a few minutes to think about the normal patterns of these people who live around you; then write down five words to describe how they typically do life every day?

Divide your words into two categories: Positive/Negative. Then create one sentence that describes how you and your neighbors do life every day. The sentence might begin this way:

The pattern of my neighbors is best described as…?

Close your gathering with prayer, asking the Holy Spirit to continue leading you in this process.

WHAT'S GOING ON IN OUR NEIGHBORHOODS?

In order to craft a mission statement that will shape your congregation's missional identity, you'll need to understand what's going on with your neighbors and within your neighborhoods. The key that helped me develop a mission statement that was easy for the emerging congregation at the Bridge to relate to was my growing understanding of what was going on in the neighborhoods around our emerging new church.

The more I shared what I was learning about our neighborhoods with the <u>Circle of Ten,</u> the more we figured out what God was at work doing and what God was calling us to do and be as a new congregation.

The more accurately you and your <u>Circle of Ten</u> (or small group planning team) can articulate what is going on in the neighborhoods around your congregation, the more clearly your congregation will understand their vocation and the more excited they will be about joining Jesus on mission.

GROUP DISCUSSION: WHAT'S GOING ON IN OUR NEIGHBORHOODS

Open your gathering with prayer, asking the Holy Spirit to bless your work and guide your conversations. Just like the previous exercise, you will need to dry erase board or some electronic means of visually sharing the results of your shared work.

Begin this part of the discernment by engaging in the following questions with your <u>Circle of Ten</u> or small group planning team. For maximum effectiveness, send your <u>Circle of Ten</u> into the community to informally ask others the questions below. Then, re-gather after a week or two to discuss what the team has learned.

Sending your <u>Circle of Ten</u> into the community doesn't have to feel awkward or contrived. Most people in your congregation are already involved in civic organizations; homeowners associations; school board activities and other groups. All your Circle of Ten needs to do is ask people in their social networks or group affiliations some of the following question.

After the <u>Circle of Ten</u> has collected the important missional intel from their social networks, re-gather to discuss the following questions.

- What needs did you discover in your neighborhood?
- What needs did you learn about in the larger city or town in which your congregation serves?
- What sort of pain/suffering do you see in your neighborhood and in the town where your congregation is located?

- Who is nobody paying attention to in your neighborhood?
- Who, in your neighborhood, does your heart break over?
- What issues or problems are causing people in your neighborhood to organize in order to address?

Spend time in your small groups sharing your thoughts and summarizing your findings in the dry erase board. Then, create one sentence that describes the needs; the pain and the marginalized in your neighborhood.[62] Your one sentence might begin either of these two ways:

1. The needs and pains in our neighborhood are best described as...
2. We see the Lord at work in our neighborhood in the following ways...

GROUP DISCUSSION: COMBINE WHAT YOU ARE LEARNING

Use a dry erase board and write down your team's responses to the question from the Exercise #1: The pattern of my neighbors is best described as...? Then write down your team's responses to the question from the second exercise: The needs and pains in our neighborhood are best described as...?

As you look at the answer to the two questions side by side, use the questions below to begin to tease out an emerging mission statement.

- Discuss what you are learning about your neighbors and neighborhoods.
- What stands out to you?
- What surprises you?

62   You may find it impossible to reduce your finds to one sentence. That's fine. The main thing is to try and be as concise as possible.

- What is needed in your neighborhoods?
- Where is the Lord at work in your neighborhoods?
- How are the needs and challenges you are uncovering being addressed by your congregation and what is not being addressed?

If possible, began crafting an initial mission statement based upon what is being revealed to you. (You may want to invite everyone in the Circle of Ten to write an emerging mission statement and then share each with the whole group).

Close your gathering with prayer, asking the Holy Spirit to continue leading you in this process.

WHAT'S GOING ON IN OUR CONGREGATION?

In order to craft a mission statement that will shape your congregation's missional identity, you need to understand your neighbors; your neighborhoods and finally your congregation. The following exercise will help you and your Circle of Ten to gain a clearer picture of how the Lord is preparing your congregation to recover its missional identity.

GROUP DISCUSSION: UNDERSTANDING OUR CONGREGATION

Open your gathering with prayer, asking the Holy Spirit to bless your work and guide your conversations. You will need a dry erase board or some electronic way of tabulating and sharing responses from the team.

Here are some questions for you and the Circle of Ten to discuss. Feel free to tweak these questions by using language that your congregation is comfortable with.

- How are we performing the gospel each week?
- How does our church do life, together?
- What are the words we would use to describe our congregation, and particularly, what words describe how we live the gospel life together?
- What is unique about our church's life together?
- Why do people join your church? Why do they stay?
- What gifts does this community possess that might be a blessing to the wider community?

After you have engaged the above questions, spend a minute in your small groups summarizing your thoughts and write words or a sentence that describes the patterns of your shared life, together. Perhaps you can answer the question by using this sentence:

The best way to describe how we perform the gospel, together, is…?

HOW TO CONNECT OUR CONGREGATION WITH OUR NEIGHBORHOOD

In order to craft a mission statement that will shape your congregation's missional identity, you will need to connect your church to your neighborhood. The final step in this process is to integrate what you and the Circle of Ten have uncovered about your neighborhoods and your congregation.

Begin by sharing with the group the answers to the questions posed in the previous exercises along with any initial attempts by the team to fashion a mission statement for your congregation. Then, use the questions below to continue the process of uncovering and crafting God's mission statement for your congregation:

- Where do the needs and pain in your neighborhoods connect with the ways you are doing life together?
- What emerging questions/challenges in your neighborhoods has your congregation already begun addressing or have the capacity to address?
- How do you see the Lord preparing your congregation to be on mission in your neighborhoods?
- What unique gifts does your congregation possess that could bless the neighborhoods around your congregation?
- How can you be Jesus in real-time to your neighbors?

After you have answered the above questions, then re-examine your first attempts at writing a mission statement from the previous discussion: Combining What You Are Learning. As a group, use what you have learned from the above questions and change, tweak or add to your team's first attempt at a mission statement.

Close your gathering with prayer, asking the Holy Spirit to continue leading you in this process.

PUTTING YOUR MISSION STATEMENT TOGETHER: ASKING THE WHAT AND WHY QUESTION

I believe every congregation should have a mission statement. I love the language authors Coalter, Mulder and Weeks use in their book The Re-Forming Tradition: Presbyterians and Mainstream Protestantism. The argue that: *"The church's community must have a forthright and compelling persuasive vision of what the church is and should be for Christian witness."*[63]

63   Milton J. Coalter, John M. Mulder and Louis B. Weeks, *The Re-Forming Tradition: Presbyterians and Mainstream Protestantism,* (Louisville: Westminster/John Knox Press,

When I started the Bridge Presbyterian Church, I wanted to craft a mission statement that would clearly answer two questions. The first is: *"What matters most around here?"* That is the question that folks are asking when they visit us for the first and second time. This means that vague statements like, "to glorify God" or *"to make disciples"* are way too generic and are run the risk of using Christian insider-language that newcomers to the faith may not understand. Churches need to be creative, specific and contextual in how they answer the question: *"What matters most around here?"*

The second question I wanted our mission statement to answer is: *"Why are we doing what we are doing?"* What is our goal? I realize that visitors to the Bridge view the church as one of many good choices to invest their time, talent and treasure. So, I want new people to the Bridge to clearly understand why the Bridge is doing what it's doing. Take a look at our mission statement:

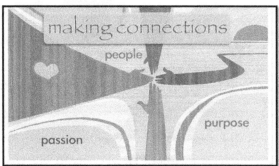

THE MISSION OF THE BRIDGE PRESBYTERIAN CHURCH IS TO HELP PEOPLE CONNECT WITH GOD'S PEOPLE, PURPOSE AND PURPOSE/ PRESENCE IN THEIR LIFE.

As you can see, we were intentional about incorporating what we learned about our neighbors into our mission statement - so that our

1992), 283-84.

mission statement clearly articulates what matters around here and the goal of our life together.

Now, it's your turn. The next step in crafting a mission statement that will shape your congregation's missional identity is to return the emerging mission statement you and your team have been working on with the help of the above exercises.

Your emerging mission statement should reflect a) what's going on in the lives of your neighbors; with b) what's happening within your neighborhood; with c) what God is doing in your congregation in a way that reveals d) how your congregations' strengths, abilities and passions align with the needs of the community. As you look at your emerging mission statement, ask the following two questions:

Does our emerging mission statement answer the question: What matters most around here? If not, then continue to edit your mission statement.

Does our emerging mission statement answer the question: Why are we doing what we are doing? If not, then continue to edit your mission statement.

As you can see, the mission statement of the Bridge Presbyterian Church shapes the rhythm of our life in ways that connect us to the needs of the neighborhood. So, when folks ask why we are doing what we are doing, the answer is simple: to join Jesus in making a difference in our neighborhood.

That said, I know that mission statements can take long time to craft and short time to be forgotten – once they are adopted by the congregation. Peter Drucker writes this about mission statements: *"A mission statement has to be operational, otherwise it's just good intentions. A mission statement has to focus on what the institution really tries to do… so that everybody in the organization can say, "This is my contribution to the goal."*

In an effort to keep the mission statement fresh and help guide all we do at the Bridge, we structured our worship service; our leadership team, as well as our missional sermon-based small groups around our mission statement. Once your mission statement has been finalized and adopted by your leadership team and congregation, you may want to consider the following ways to use your new mission statement to help guide your congregation.

We decided to use the three-part mission statement to guide our worship life at the Bridge Presbyterian Church. You will find an example of a Sunday order of worship in the appendix section. You will see how we divided our worship service into three seamless transitions. Each transition highlights one of the three connections used in our mission statement.

Secondly, we decided to use our mission statement to structure our small-group study guides. We divide our missional sermon-based small groups into three seamless transitions reflecting our mission statement. You will find an example of how we structure our small-group study guide in chapter two.

EPILOGUE

Long before the Pandemic radically altered the Church, it was clear that things needed to change. The pandemic not only accelerated that need but gave pastors and church leaders legitimate reason to invite their worshiping communities to change. I believe missional sermon-based small groups are a faithful and compelling way for the church to morph. But change in any institution is difficult and change within the local church may be more challenging than in other institutions.

While renewal in the local church may seem obvious and captivating, the opportunity for change and renewal carries with it risks, challenges and certain opposition. As you prayerfully consider the urgency and the hazards of leading change within your congregation, I invite you to lean into the words of author Eugene Peterson.

In Matthew 11: 28 – 30 we read: "Come to me, all you that are weary and are carrying heavy burdens, and I will give you rest. ²Take my yoke upon you, and learn from me; for I am gentle and humble in heart, and you will find rest for your souls. ³For my yoke is easy, and my burden is light."

Commenting this passage, Peterson writes: "The day teems with possibilities. Jesus' command rouses us out of a sleepy timidity…(Jesus) calls us into a yoked companionship with himself. He doesn't ask us to do anything that he doesn't promise to do with us. We are not so much sent out as invited along."[64]

I pray that Peterson's comments will inspire and sustain you as you join in Jesus' work in the world and in your congregation. I want to thank you for reading my book. I leave you with a prayer I wrote based on the words from Matthew 3:11-12 (The Message translation) May this be your prayer as you follow our living and reigning Lord. God bless!

"Lord, I thank you that you are igniting a passion within me, a fire

---

64   Peterson, A Year with Jesus, 117.

within me, the Holy Spirit within me, changing me from the inside out. You are going to clean house, make a clean sweep of my life! I thank you for the changes you are making because those changes are saving me, everyday! (Matthew 3:12)

APPENDICES

APPENDIX A

MISSIONAL SERMON-BASED SMALL GROUP LEADERS GUIDE

OUR PURPOSE:

The purpose of our Sermon-Based Small Groups is: To deepen the three connections in our mission statement:

- To connect with God's passion for our life;
- To connect with God's people in our life;
- To connect with God's purpose for our life.

OUR VISION:

Participating in small groups is the primary way adults learn and grow in their faith. Participating in small groups is the primary way members of The Bridge live out our mission statement. We have chosen the Sermon-Based Small Group Model for the following reasons:

1. It's so easy to participate in or lead. All you have to do is attend worship (or read the sermon on line if you miss Sunday worship).
2. It helps make Sunday worship a priority at The Bridge.
3. It is an easy way to involve seekers who aren't ready to come to Sunday worship, but who are looking for Christ and a church home.

OUR STRUCTURE:

Each Sermon-Based Small Group will be led by an **individual leader** or **lead couple**. The **leader(s)** are responsible for:

- Preparing to lead the discussion.
- Making sure everyone has a bible.
- Collecting requests/celebrations and praying for the group.
- Working with Doug to provide care for crisis or emergencies that emerge in the group.

Each SBSS should plan on meeting for 60 - 75 minutes.

Connecting with God's People in our life (20 minutes)

- Greeting Participants
- Informal visiting, sharing, getting to know one another

Connecting with God's Passion for our life (40-45 minutes)

- Go through the study guide
- End by sharing prayer concerns/celebrations

Connecting with God's Purpose for our life

- Plan to participate in a mission project (voluntary) that the Mission Team suggests. The project should be completed by the end of the study. Have someone take pictures of hands-on projects.

OUR COVENANT:

I agree to meet every week at the appointed time for the duration of the SBSG unless I'm traveling or have an emergency and cannot attend.

I also agree to come prepared for the study either by worshipping on Sunday morning or by reading the sermon.

Finally, I agree to pray for the members of this study on a regular basis and I agree to bring a Bible if I'm able.

TIPS & LOGISTICS FOR LEADING SERMON-BASED SMALL GROUPS

Logistics:

- Doug will always have the study guide ready by Friday (if not sooner). Doug will email the study ahead of Sunday worship.
- Doug will always post the sermon before he leaves church on Sunday morning.
- You are encouraged to take notes during the sermon if you feel this will be helpful when leading the study.

Tips for Leading:

Begin your preparation time and your leadership time with prayer asking the Holy Spirit to lead you.

- Doug always creates more questions than needed. **Don't feel you need to engage every question**. Go with the flow. Stay with the questions that the group is focused on.
- Resist the temptation to talk when there is silence in the room. After you have teed up the question let the group wrestle with how they will answer it. Don't be **uncomfortable with** silence.
- Remember that the group is getting to know each other. They will, likely feel inhibited for a while until they are comfortable with the group.
- Thank people for their contributions and questions.
- Don't feel you need to know the answers. If a question emerges you can't answer simply ask the group for their feedback. If necessary, say to the group: "I'll ask Doug this question and get back to you."
- Encourage people to bring guests.
- Sometimes people will want to discuss what's going on in their faith journey. Encourage that and **balance it with staying on task**. Part of the goal is to connect with each other.
- Ask the group to agree to the following covenant (if possible):
- What is said in the group stays in the group.

- We will commit to creating a safe place for everyone to share freely.
- Keeping casting the vision: Remind participants that our mission statement consists of making three connections in small groups.

APPENDIX B

MISSIONAL SERMON-BASED SMALL GROUP FAQ'S

SERMON BASED SMALL GROUPS

WHAT ARE MISSIONAL SERMON-BASED SMALL GROUPS AT THE *BRIDGE* PRESBYTERIAN CHURCH

Small groups are a really important part of the *Bridge Presbyterian Church*. A new round of small groups will kick off the week of January 18th. Here are some *Frequently Asked Questions* about small groups at *the Bridge*.

What's the purpose of small groups at the *Bridge*?

The **Bridge** is growing rapidly. At the **Bridge,** small groups are where friendships form; care for each other is given; people pray and do mission together.

Small Groups are the primary way to study God's Word at the **Bridge**. Think of small groups as Sunday school 2.0.

Participating in small groups is a non-threatening way for people who aren't ready for Sunday worship to connect with the **Bridge.**

What Are Sermon Based Small Groups at the *Bridge*?

Sermon-Based Small Groups meet weekly to discuss the theme and bible passages used in the sermon the previous Sunday.

Sermon-Based Small Groups studies are written by Dr. Doug. Each 60 – 90 minute study provides time for: 1) connecting with God's people through fellowship and food; 2) connecting with God's passion through study and prayer; 3) connecting with God's purpose through focused discussed on how the group can do local mission, together.

Why Sermon Based Small Groups at the *Bridge*?

SBSG's are easy! There is NO preparation for leaders or participants. Just show up and listen to the sermon!

SBSG's increase worship attendance!

SBSG's create dynamic spiritual growth!

SBSG's provide hands on ministry!

SBSG's provide a great way to get to know people and the Bible!

SBSG's provide opportunities to care for each other!

Nuts and Bolts of Sermon-Based Small Groups at the Bridge.

This round of SBSG will last 11 weeks.

SBSG's meet either in home or at the worship center

SBSG's consist of 1-2 facilitators and 6 – 12 participants who rotate snacks/hosting as they are able.

Each participant will be given the study prior to Sunday worship. The study can be used to take notes.

New groups form quarterly. Nobody has to stay in the same small group.

Each small group will decide and participate in a mission project during the length of the small group. The project can be an existing one or a new project the group comes up with.

What are the goals for small groups at the Bridge?

One goal is to have 50% of the Bridge involved in a small group.

Another goal is to have most of the mission and ministry at the Bridge done through small groups.

This year, different types of small groups will emerge allowing various ways for people to meet and connect with God's passion, people and purpose.

How can you get involved in small groups at the Bridge?

Soon there will be two Sundays to sign up for small groups at the **Bridge.**

Once signed up, you will be contacted and given directions for how to get to your small group. You will also receive the first study guide as soon as you sign up.

APPENDIX C

SAMPLE SIGN-UP SHEET MISSIONAL SERMON-BASED SMALL GROUPS

WHO: Everyone at the Bridge!

WHEN: January 18th – March 29th

WHERE: In homes and at the Bridge.

NEEDS:

_____ I can facilitate = Facilitators lead the discussion each week Optional…find a co-facilitator

_____ I can host: Hosts = Open your home to 8 – 10 people once a week for 12 weeks.

_____ I'll be a Participant = Sermon-Based Small Groups are the BEST way to connect with God's people, passion and purpose for your life and the best way to get involved with God's mission at the Bridge.

APPENDIX D

MISSIONAL SERMON-BASED SMALL GROUP STUDY GUIDE

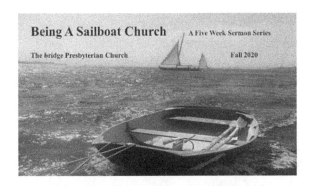

BEING A SAILBOAT CHURCH: I

CONNECTING WITH GOD'S PEOPLE

<u>Getting to Know Each Other:</u>

Welcome to our fall 2020 Sermon-Based Small Groups at the Bridge! Spend some time getting to know each other in your small group (if you don't already know each other). Share with the group your name and where you live.

Or share with the group an experience you've had either sailing or rowing in a rowboat. Where were you? What was that like? Where were you going?

CONNECTING WITH GOD'S PASSION

Digging Deeper

1. What insight, principle, or observation from this weekend's message did you find to be most helpful, eye-opening, or troubling? Explain.

2. The earliest Christians chose a sailboat as a symbol for the church, because the earliest followers of Jesus understood that the Church was a God-powered, God-led and God-equipped adventure and the only way to be in relationship with Jesus, together, was by hoisting a sail and allowing themselves to be taken wherever the Lord wanted to take them.

- How do you react to the idea of our life together at the Bridge as an adventure with God?

- Discuss the differences that author Joan Gray points out below between a Sailboat Church and a Rowboat Church

The Rowboat Church

Attitude = Either "WE can or WE can't do what God has called US to do."

Progress = "Depends on circumstances like how much money do WE have or where is OUR location."

Focus = "What can WE do with what WE have?"

The Sailboat Church

Attitude = "GOD can do infinitely more than we can ask or imagine."

Progress = "Because God leads and empowers us, what we lack in resources is not decisive to what God can accomplish in us.

Focus = "What is God leading us to be and do now in the place where we find ourselves?"

3. READ John 15: 1-11: In John 15, Jesus uses an organic metaphor of being engrafted by the Father into the central vine, which is Jesus Christ.

- Share with the group any observations or questions you have. How does this metaphor help you understand what it means to 'abide in Jesus?'

- Central to the notion of 'abiding in Jesus' is the idea of being dependent upon our Lord, like a branch to a vine. How can the Bridge faithfully live in the tension between depending on Jesus yet not sitting idly by and doing nothing?

4. As Sailboat Churches abide with Jesus, the true vine, they learn how to let the Lord shape their desires; their decisions and their actions.

- Give examples of how has the Lord shaped your desires and decisions throughout your life?

- Give examples of how and where you see the Lord shaping the desires and decisions of the Bridge Presbyterian Church?

5. John 15: 5: *"I am the vine, you are the branches. Those who abide in me and I in them bear much fruit, because apart from me you can do nothing."* What does Jesus mean when he said: *"Apart from me you can do nothing?"* What difference would it make in your life if you took very seriously these words of Jesus?

6. John 15:6. NRSV: *"Whoever does not abide in me is thrown away like a branch and withers; such branches are gathered, thrown into the fire, and burned."* People in Sailboat Churches abide in Jesus and bear fruit or they get pruned and discarded. Where do you see the Bridge bearing fruit? How might the Lord be pruning the Bridge?

7. In marinas all around the world there are boats that seldom leave the dock. They remain tied up there, perhaps used as places to entertain or relax, even to live on, but their sails are rarely raised.

- How is the Bridge like a boat tied up in a marina and how is the

Bridge like sailboat that has caught the wind of the Holy Spirit?

- How do you see the Bridge partnering with God? How do you experience yourself as a partner with God in God's work in the world?

Personal Application:

1. Doug ended the sermon with a call to recover the sailing life, challenging everyone to take three simple steps toward abiding with Jesus. Take time to consider (or discuss) each of the three steps:

- First, abide in Jesus by joining a small group.
- Second, pray. Pray for the Bridge; it's leaders; and for the leading of the Holy Spirit.
- Third, let go of your agendas and dreams for the Bridge and with renewed trust and dependence on the Holy Spirit, hoist the sails and follow where the wind leads.

2. Prayerfully consider how you can become more of a sailor and less of a rower in your spiritual life. Prayerfully consider how the Bridge can, together, become more of a Sailboat Church and less of a Rowboat Church.

CONNECTING WITH GOD'S PURPOSE

Our September featured Mission Partners: Matthew's Ministry and Charter Day School of Roger Bacon Academy. Matthew's Ministry provides food for local children so they have nourishment on weekends. Back-packs are needed to send the groceries home with them. The Bridge sponsors Town Creek Elementary and Charter Day School.

Charter Day School is in need of loose-leaf paper, one subject notebooks, glue sticks, pencil pouches, and erasers. If you feel called to support these ministries, a bin will be provided for your donations Monday, September 28, from 10:00-11:00 a.m.in front of the Bridge.

Monetary donations may be sent to the Bridge Presbyterian Church, 497 Olde Waterford Way,

Suite 205, Leland, NC, 28451, with "Matthew's Ministry" or "Charter Day School" on the memo line.

APPENDIX E

SAMPLE OF ORDER OF WORSHIP

the bridge
presbyterian church
www.thebridgepres.org

February 17, 2017

CONNECTING WITH GOD'S PEOPLE

Welcome

Singing Praise to God

    Lord Reign in Me

    Leaning on the Everlasting Arms

Prayer of Confession

CONNECTING WITH GOD'S PASSION

Gathering Around God's Word

    Prayer

Scripture: Psalms 49:16-20; Matthew 6:19-21; James 1:9-11

Sermon: Who Tells You Who You Are?

Offering

    The Lord's Supper

CONNECTING WITH GOD'S PURPOSE

    How to get involved in Matthew's Ministry

Singing Praise to God

    I Surrender All

Benediction

BIBLIOGRAPHY

Bolsinger, Tod. *Tempered Resilience: How Leaders Are Formed in the Crucible of Change*. Downers Grove: Intervarsity Press, 2022.

Boren, M. Scott Boren. *Missional Small Groups: Becoming A Community That Makes a Difference in the World*. Grand Rapids: Baker Books, 2010.

Cushing, Doug. *Where There's No Road at All: Adventures in Church Planting*. Columbia: Pinnacle Leadership Press, 2013.

Dennison, Charles. *Mainline Manifesto: The Inevitable New Church*. St. Louis: Charlice Press, 2005.

Frankl, Victor. *Man's Search for Meaning*. Boston: Beacon Press, 1959.

Frazee, Randy. *Making Room for Life*. Grand Rapids: Zondervan, 2004.

Coalter, Milton, John Mulder and Louis Weeks. *The Re-Forming Tradition: Presbyterians and Mainstream Protestantism*. Louisville: Westminster/John Knox Press, 1992.

Cole, Diane. "A Message From Your Brain: I'm Not Good at Remembering What I Hear." *National Geographic*, March 13, 2014. https://www.nationalgeographic.com/science/article/140312-auditory-memory-visual-learning-brain-research-science.

Gray, Joan. *Sailboat Church: Helping Your Church Rethink Its Mission and Practice*. Louisville: Westminster John Knox Press, 2014.

Gilbert, Daniel. *Stumbling on Happiness*. New York: Vantage Books, 2005.

Guder, Darrell. *Missional Church: A Vision for the Sending of the Church in North America*. Grand Rapids: Eerdmans, 1998.

Halter, Hugh and Matt Smay. *The Tangible Kingdom Primer*. Gig Harbor: Missio Publishing, 2009.

Halter, Hugh and Matt Smay. *And: The Gathered and Scattered Church*. Grand Rapids: Zondervan, 2010.

Hartnett, Kelly. "Your Church is More Than a Worship Service: Finding Other On-Ramps." *Church Marketing Sucks*. September 10, 2014, http://churchmarketingsucks.com/2014/09/your-church-is-more-than-a-worship-service-finding-other-on-ramps/

Lipka, Michael and Claire Gecewicz, "More Americans Now Say They're Spiritual But Not Religious." *Pew Research Center*. September 6, 2017. http://www.pewresearch.org/fact-tank/2017/09/06/more-americans-now-say-theyre-spiritual-but-not-religious/

Manatrea, Milfred. *Shaped By God's Heart: The Passion and Practices of Missional Churches*. Hoboken, Jossey Bass, 2010.

Marnell, Jameson. "C'Mon Get Happy." *LA Times*, September 8, 2008.

McSpadden, Kevin. "You Now Have a Shorter Attention Span Than a Goldfish." *Time*, May 14, 2015. https://time.com/3858309/attention-spans-goldfish/

Nortey, Justin. "More Houses of Worship Are Returning to Normal, But In-Person Worship Remains Unchanged Since Fall." *Pew Research Center*, March 22, 2022. <https://www.pewresearch.org/fact-tank/2022/03/22/more-houses-of-worship-are-returning-to-normal-operations-but-in-person-attendance-is-unchanged-since-fall/#:~:text=In%20July%202020%2C%20roughly%20four,and%20now%20stands%20at%2027%25

Osborne, Larry. *Sticky Church*. Grand Rapids: Zondervan, 2008.

Osterhaus, James, Joseph M. Jurkowski and Todd A. Hahn. *Thriving Through Ministry Conflict by Understanding Your Red and Blue Zones*. Grand Rapids: Zondervan, 2005.

Peterson, Eugene. *A Year with Jesus: Daily Readings and Meditations*. New York: Harper Collins, 2006.

Peterson, Eugene. *Reversed Thunder*. New York: Harper Collins, 1998.

Pink, Daniel. *Drive: The Surprising Truth About What Motivates Us*. New York: Penguin Group, 2011.

Purves, Andrew. *The Crucifixion of Ministry: Surrendering Our Ambition to the Service of Christ*. Downers Grove: InterVarsity Press, 2007.

Rubin, Gretchen. *The Happiness Project*. New York: Harper Collins, 2018.

Rugaber, Christopher, S. "Ben Bernanke Has A Question for You: Are you Happy?" *NBCNews.com*, August 10, 2012. http://economywatch.nbcnews.com/_news/2012/08/06/13148811-ben-bernanke-has-a-question-for-you-are-you-happy?lite

Senior, Deborah, "Some Dark Thoughts on Happiness." *New York Magazine*, July 17, 2006. https://nymag.com/news/features/17573/

Smith, Emily Esfahani and Jennifer L. Aaker, "Millennial Searchers." *New York Times*, Nov 30, 2013.

Tidsworth, Mark. *SHIFT; Three Big Moves For the 21st Century Church*. Columbia: Pinnacle Leadership Press, 2015.

Vaughn, Patrick. *Meeting Jesus at Starbucks: Good News for Those Done With Church*. Columbia: Pinnacle Leadership Press, 2018.

Zakarin, Jordan. "Steven Spielberg Reveals Daniel Day Lewis Original 'Lincoln' Rejection Letter." *The Hollywood Reporter*. January 8, 2013. https://www.hollywoodreporter.com/news/general-news/steven-spielberg-reveals-daniel-day-409709/ .

ABOUT THE AUTHOR

Dr. Doug Cushing is the Founding Pastor and Head of Staff of the Bridge Presbyterian Church in Leland, NC. Doug was born and raised outside of Milwaukee, WI. He attended Carroll College earning B.S. degrees in Clinical Psychology and Communications. Doug earned a Master of Arts in Christian Thought from Trinity Divinity School; a Master of Divinity from Princeton Theological Seminary and a Doctor of Ministry with specialization in Church Planting from Columbia Theological Seminary.

An ordained minister in the Presbyterian Church, USA, Doug has served churches in Chicago, Philadelphia and, most recently, in the Upstate of South Carolina where he served as Founding Pastor and then Head of Staff of the Tyger River Presbyterian Church.

Doug is also a coach and consultant for new church pastors with Pinnacle Leadership Associates. In 2016, Doug published his first book: Where There's No Road At All: Adventures in Church Planting. For the past 15 years, Doug has served as a PCUSA certified coach for new churches and church planters. He has coached and consulted church planting projects in Minnesota; Ohio; Georgia; Tennessee and the Carolinas. He has taught about his experiences in church planting in Baghdad, Iraq and Columbia Seminary.

Doug and his wife Sharon live in Leland, NC along with their two-year old Cocker Spaniel named Coji. They both enjoy scuba diving, sailing, traveling and watching the Green Bay Packers – of which Doug is a part owner of the team.

Doug can be reached at 52drdoug@gmail.com.

CPSIA information can be obtained
at www.ICGtesting.com
Printed in the USA
JSHW021207130623
43138JS00003B/206